The Dog Friendly Book - Gloucestershire and the Cotswolds

Rachael Wyatt

Find out more at:

www.dogfriendlybook.co.uk

Published by:

Whitehill Publishing

Beaumont Enterprise Centre

72, Boston Road, Beaumont Leys

Leicester LE4 1HB

Tel: 0116 2293102 Fax: 0116 2351844

www.whitehillpublishing.org.uk

ISBN 978-1-291-34939-9

Whitehill publishing has used its best efforts in collecting analysing and preparing material for inclusion in this directory.

It does not assume, and hereby disclaims and liability to any party, for any loss or damage cause by errors or omissions in this guide, whether such errors or omissions result from negligence, accident or other cause.

For Ida Emma

Contents

Introducing Skateboard..4
Before we start..7
Things to Do..10
The Forest of Dean...11
Winchcombe, Tewkesbury & Broadway..............25
Cheltenham...41
Gloucester 50
Stroud & Area..58
South Cotswolds..79
North Cotswolds...95

Introduction to Places to Stay...........................115
Forest of Dean - Places to Stay..........................116
Winchcombe, Tewkesbury & Broadway - Places to
Stay..123
Cheltenham - Places to Stay...............................131
Gloucester - Places to Stay.................................136
Stroud & Area - Places to Stay............................140
South Cotswolds - Places to Stay.......................147
North Cotswolds - Places to Stay.......................152

Appendices:
Emergency Numbers - Vets & Dog Wardens......166
About Hearing Dogs for Deaf People...................174

Introducing Skateboard

Back in November 2006, a lurcher puppy was born in a shed in Didcot. There were no stars and no wise men, but upon hearing that the lurcher had been born, an Idiot set out on a journey to visit her. The Idiot knew that when you are faced with a litter of puppies you are supposed to choose the strongest, most robust, sociable puppy. Instead she chose the quiet little thing who seemed overwhelmed by the writhing mass of wags, and the needle sharp teeth of her brothers and sisters. She sat quietly observing the Idiot from the safety of her hiding place behind the sofa. And so it was that this quiet little scrap was the first one to leave the litter with what seemed to be a palpable relief.

Unfortunately The Idiot had only mentioned to her partner that she and The Boy were 'going to look at some puppies' and had definitely not mentioned that there was a dog crate, some house training pads, two bowls, a collar and a bag of puppy kibble in the boot of the car.

The puppy quickly settled into The Boy's lap and fell in to such a deep contented sleep that about a mile from Oxford the boy said

"Mum, seriously, stop the car - it's stopped breathing"

'It' hadn't. 'It' was simply demonstrating its uncanny ability to switch between two very separate states of consciousness: 'awake' with all the various subsets of playful, hungry, naughty, devious and barking like a loon, and what appeared to be 'coma'.

Less than a mile from home The Idiot began to vocalise the nagging thought that had been with her for a while. This might be a bad thing. A very bad thing.

Settling the puppy in (and warning The Boy that it might be going back in the morning) The Idiot drove to the office to break the 'good news' to her partner who declared himself 'a bit disappointed', sighed, packed up his laptop and made his way home. Entering the living room his only comment was

"There's a dog on *my* chair".

He picked the puppy up like a bachelor holding a newborn, sat down and placed her on his lap, where she immediately made herself comfortable by snuggling into the crook of his arm and demonstrating 'coma' mode again.

"We're going to call her Skateboard" he said.

The Idiot's mouth opened slightly in protest, but then she realised that if we were naming it, we were definitely keeping it.

My name is Rachael and yes, sometimes I am a bit of an idiot.

Jack (aka The Boy) and I had been bellyaching for a dog for months before the trip out to see the puppies. Boy had promised that he would walk a dog every day if we got one, and promptly left home before she was even a year old.

We were very lucky. We run our own business so we were able to take the dog to work with us every day where she'd spent most of the time sleeping, some of the time mithering for a walk when we really needed to concentrate, and once famously got herself tangled in a floor standing fan, bringing it crashing to the floor and causing such a commotion and yelping so loudly that the other businesses in the office block were convinced we'd been trying to cut off her tail with a rusty spoon.

My main motivation for wanting a dog was the notion that she would make a great companion, and help me by hearing for me. I've been going deaf since my mid 20's and I figured that having a dog would help alert me to the things I could no longer hear. The local puppy training class was run by an ex hearing dogs instructor, so I'd hoped that she'd spot something special about Skateboard and help me to train her to hear the phone, warn me of impending danger and indicate to people that I wasn't rude, I was just very deaf.

And indeed, the instructor did spot something special in Skateboard. After 3 weeks they had to start shutting the windows in the church hall due to her determination to escape by jumping out of them. She took to puppy training and socialisation in the same way that Wayne Sleep would take to rugby union. Week one was relatively uneventful, week two was slightly less successful. Taking advantage of an unnoticed puddle of wee, a huge black Labrador dragged it's helpless owner across the wooden floor, cornered Skateboard and bit her on the bum. I burst into tears.

Each Wednesday I'd get her lead out and she'd be doing the walk 'ruhruhruh' until the minute we got to the junction of the road with the church hall, then she'd start pulling in the opposite direction. But we persevered. She graduated, and we started to meet and play with other dogs on the local dog walking field. Unfortunately, weeks apart, she was attacked in two separate incidents. The last one involved her running home with a border terrier hot on her heels. It was still wearing the extending lead its owner had failed to keep hold of, and we could only watch helplessly as the heavy handle pinged off the parked cars either side of the road.

Pretty soon it became clear that she was going to be a mainly 'lead on' dog and the assistance vest was a distant dream. We needed to find some places where we could take her, and that's when we started writing this.

We decided that we wanted to put together a useful guide not only for people who were visiting Gloucestershire, but also for people who lived here and simply didn't know about the huge range of things you can do with your dog in tow... because it's fair to say that until we started researching this we had a pretty limited repertoire of things to do and places to visit.

In short - we've had terrible days out so you don't have to.

Before we start

We're going to assume that you are sensible dog owners and you don't need us to pad the guide out with useful tips about travelling with dogs, the importance of insurance and the country code - however some of our guide books do have information about beaches and bylaws in the appendix.

How the guide is set out

We've tried to do it as logically as we can, so it's basically in three sections: Sections 1 and 2 are split by areas that seem to make sense to us (but then calling a dog Skateboard seemed to make sense to us). We didn't want to duplicate information, so we've highlighted other attractions that may be close but in another section of the book. You'll also notice little stories and anecdotes dotted throughout the book - this is because I'm a massive show off and frustrated novelist and Skateboard does stupid stuff that I just want to write about - in fact her full name should probably be 'Oh For Goodness Sake Skateboard'. That's the polite version.

A quick note about Hearing Dogs for Deaf People.

As I already mentioned I'm gradually losing my hearing. Technically I'd qualify for a hearing dog. However, the waiting list is very very long and I'm not altogether sure what I'd do with a well trained, attentive, intelligent dog, so we're sticking with Skatie. Some people are not so 'lucky' and don't have a Skateboard in their lives, and that's why a proportion of the profits of this book will be going to Hearing Dogs for Deaf People. You can read a bit more about them in the appendix.

1. Places to go

This includes walks, museums, days out and places to eat. If there's a dog friendly pub near an attraction, we'll tell you about it. There's also a selection of walks with dog friendly pubs en route. We've also tried to find as many non-pub places to eat as possible, although we admit to a slight 'pub' preference (ahem..)

About the walks we mention

I was on the phone to my friend Gerry

"We loved the Lake District. Do you fancy going up there? You and Greg can fish and maybe Ness and I can do a few walks?"

The very mention of the W word starts Skateboard angling for a walk, making the ruhruhruh noise that Lurchers are so good at whilst running between the front door and her lead. Whilst it's cute and funny it also means that we have to be very careful what we say.

We've tried every variation of the W word, including spelling it. Made up words like 'Bimble', worked for less than 3 months, the 'yellow pages finger walking sign thing' even less. It's now got to the point where she can be in the deepest sleep and if she hears the phrase 'Would you like?..' her eyes stay closed but her ears prick up immediately to check that none of the walk 'code words' are mentioned. Tell me dogs can't spell and I will prove you wrong, tell me they can't count and I will tell you of the night where we ran out of biscuits and she only got two, not three before bed.

Did we sleep?

You have a dog, right?

Anyway - the walks.....

We noticed that some of the reviews of other Dog Friendly books in the UK often mentioned that there were no pictures of walks or detailed instructions. What we've tried to do is stick to walks we would do - that is - marked paths and trails. We've done this because we realised that many of the people who come to the Cotswolds for walking holidays will have the walks they want to do planned already, and what we're trying to provide is a range of activities you can do with your dog - not JUST walking. Another reason we tend to stick to way-marked walks is that having a skittish scaredy lurcher doesn't really lend itself to being distracted by a map, whilst she's chased over a field by a scary looking Yorkshire terrier. Walking Skateboard off lead means being aware of possible danger at all times. Even if it **is** just a hard looking squirrel or a mixy rabbit.

2. Places to stay

We figure that finding things to do and finding accommodation are largely unrelated activities unless you *like* the frisson of a week away with no accommodation booked... and of course if you actually *live* in Gloucestershire, then you're going to be more interested in the former than the latter.

I know it's common sense, but we're finding more places are changing their dog friend-ly status because of 'bad experiences' - I know you won't let me down - or all the other dog owners who would really like a holiday with their dog. Because we live in Glouces-tershire we don't have a lot of demand for places to stay - although my parents have stayed in a couple and have written reviews. We're hoping to add more reader reviews in the second edition, so if you find a gem, let us know.

3. Appendices

Useful stuff like emergency numbers for vets and dog wardens, beach by-laws and anything else. You'll find a few independent pet shops listed in the appendices of some of our books.

Don't forget that we do a draw every month - if you visit one of the places in our guide then send us a review to editor@dogfriendlybook.co.uk. We pick 3 out of the hat each month and send £10 Amazon vouchers to the winners - so if you think our book is rub-bish you can buy a different one. By sending us a review you accept that we may choose to use it on a subsequent release of the guide - and if it's a bad one we may well take the listing out if we get more than one duff review.

Got your poo bags? lead? treats? Then let's crack on. Where do you want to go to-day?....

Things to Do

There are some activities that are not 'area specific' - and we guessed you don't want to the same activity listed over and over again, so we're listing these separately.

Geocaching

If you're not familiar with geocaching (basically a massive multi-player treasure hunt where you find and log objects hidden by fellow geocachers) then Gloucestershire is a great place to learn more, as there are thousands of geocache treasures hidden around the area. Check www.geocaching.com.

Treasure trails

We found a number of treasure trails for sale in various Tourist Information Centres we visited, so rather than listing them separately (which would be cheating really) we thought it'd be a good idea to give them a mention right here so you can have a look before you set off on your trip. If there are none for sale in the TIC, visit the website www.treasuretrails.co.uk. You'll find trails for most of the major towns in the area, and they're a great way to explore.

Walks in Gloucestershire

You'll find a selection of downloadable walks here: www.walkinginglos.co.uk/walks. php. On the whole we've tried to stick to simple way-marked walks, purely and simply because most 'proper' walkers have their own walking guide books and maps, and if you're anything like us you want simple enjoyable walks on a 'non walking' holiday. However - if you plan ahead a bit, there are plenty of free-to-download walks to access before you head off on holiday - or if you have wifi at your hotel/B&B, you can download them in the evenings. Where any downloadable walks pass dog friendly pubs we've tried to highlight them - however we haven't done all the walks, so can't guarantee that they are still passable - these are for information only.

Explore Gloucestershire iPhone app

Go to the app store and search for "explore Gloucestershire", to download the free app giving you a comprehensive 'what's on' list as well as circular walks.

The Forest of Dean

See Gloucester section for Longhope

If you're a big fan of woods then you're going to chuffing well love the Forest of Dean; more wood than you can shake a stick at. It's perfect for outdoor adventure lovers. You can take your pick from walking, cycling, canoeing, climbing - all dog friendly. If it's raining then how about a trip on the Dean Valley Railway and a leisurely pub lunch?

If you're planning on heading deep into the forest, make sure you check out the signs whatever time of year you visit, as there are wild boar roaming free in the forest. You'll need to know what to do if you're lucky enough to stumble across them (especially if they have young with them).

Wye Valley Tourism arrange a number of guided walks throughout the year on their website: www.ftg.org.uk/index.htm. You can find out more by emailing them on bookings@wyedeantourguides.org.uk

There's also a booklet of 12 easy walks which can be downloaded from the Wye Dean tourism website here: www.wyedeantourism.co.uk/files/EasyWalks.pdf

Things to do in the North of the Forest

Soudley Ponds Nature reserve

How to find it: From Soudley take the minor road to Littledean

Surfaced paths around the ponds and a walk up the ridge to the Blaize valley viewpoint. No toilets on site.

Aunt Martha's Victorian Tea-rooms

Brook Cottage, The Branch

Drybrook, Gloucestershire. GL17 9DB

Telephone: 01594 824514

Website: www.auntmartha.co.uk

Although dogs are not allowed inside, the outside of Aunt Martha's has been transformed into a selection of garden 'rooms'.

Open Fridays - 12pm - 2:30pm, Saturdays - 12pm - 5pm. Sundays - 12pm - 5pm. Usually closed out of season, so it's best to ring and check before making a trip.

Courtfield Arms

Ross Road, Lower Lydbrook, Gloucestershire. GL17 9NU

Telephone: 01594 860207

Website: www.thecourtfieldarms.co.uk

Traditional pub menu, with mains around the £10 mark.

Food served Monday - Friday 12pm - 2:30pm and 6pm - 9pm. Weekends 12pm - 9pm. Closed Monday - Thursday in Winter - Normal hours again from early March.

The George Hotel

The George Hotel, 21-23 Church Street, Newent, Gloucestershire. GL18 1PU

Telephone: 01531 820203

Website: www.georgehotel.uk.com

Dogs are welcome in the bar area.

Food served 12pm - 2pm and 6pm - 9pm.

Places to eat near walks

Yew Tree Inn & Mayhill Viewpoint

Cliffords Mesne, Newent, Gloucestershire. GL18 1JS

Telephone: 01531 820719

Website: www.yewtreeinn.com

After taking in the views from the Mayhill viewpoint, a trip to the Yew Tree will help you replenish those lost calories.... Gastro style menu, with mains around the £14 mark, as well as a good light bites menu and daily specials.

Food served Wednesday - Saturday 12pm - 2:30pm (last food orders 2pm) and 6pm - 11pm (last food orders 9pm) and Sunday lunch: 12pm - 4pm. Closed on Mondays and no lunches served on Tuesdays.

Mayhill itself has a number of way-marked paths to the summit - it's Gloucestershire's highest natural viewpoint and on a clear day you'll be able to see the Welsh Mountains, the Malvern Hills and the River Severn.

Things to do in Coleford

Beechenhurst Lodge Visitor Centre

Beechenhurst Lodge, Broadwell, Coleford, Gloucestershire. GL16 7EG

How to find it: Travelling from Coleford to Cinderford on the B4226, continue by the junction with the B4234 (Parkend to Lydbrook road) driving up the Speech House Road for 500m, before turning left into Beechenhurst.

Website: www.forestry.gov.uk

Open every day except Xmas day. Parking costs £3 - £3.50 depending on the season, but it's an all day pass to any Forestry Commission property so you can combine a visit to Beechenhurst and Symonds Yat Rock, which is what we did.

Information Centre - Beechenhurst Gift shop - Forest Connections

Telephone: 01594 822612

Website: www.forestconnections.co.uk

Dogs are welcome in the gift shop (Forest Connections) as the floor in the newly refurbished visitor centre has been specially treated to repel muck. You can buy maps of the way-marked walks (which in hindsight we wish we'd done).

You'll find a water bowl out between the cafe and the information centre, but it gets emptied very quickly due to the sheer number of doggy visitors.

Unfortunately only assistance dogs are allowed in the cafe and there is currently no covered seating, so if it's a cold or rainy day then you're best getting your cuppa at the Speech House Hotel which you can walk to through the woods. The food at the visitor centre is OK although a little expensive for what it is (£5.50 for a breakfast roll that was one egg, one slice of bacon and a sausage cut in two, along with a cup of tea).

You'll find 3 way-marked trails, and you can also walk up to the Speech House through the woods on a marked pathway to the right of the coach parking (the information centre will tell you how to find it) or walk to the Cyril Hart Arboretum.

We did the sculpture trail, as we were scoping it out for a sponsored walk for a friend. It's well signposted but a bit confusing when you get sent down a path then have to turn around and go back the way you came, because it's taken you to see a sculpture and isn't part of the 'route'. If you're a keen photographer then make sure you have your camera as the light coming through the trees is fabulous (even in February).

One tiny criticism; (and it is tiny) there are not many dog poo bins (and we didn't see any on our route but we did see some people throwing full bags over fences - shame on you!). As Skateboard tends to like to get that bit out of the way at the beginning of her walk, I ended up carrying a two bagger for 2 miles...

The Adventure Tower

Telephone: 01594 861762

Also at the Beechenhurst visitor centre (on the left as you drive in) is the Adventure tower. Described as "13m of crazy climbing and abseiling" there are 36 colour coded climbs and 2 abseils. Open 11am - 5pm in the school holidays, and weekends from April until October. Available for advanced group bookings all year round.

Cyril Hart Arboretum

Short trail around the arboretum (0.6 miles) which, although not way-marked, is easy to follow and also wheelchair/pushchair accessible. The arboretum has its own carpark (go past the entrance to Beechenhurst lodge and it's a bit further along on the left).

Symonds Yat Rock

How to find it: Signposted from Coleford

If you're a keen birdwatcher or just love amazing views then a visit here is a must. There are three way-marked walks. Follow the yellow route if you want to walk down to the dog friendly Saracens Head Inn for food.

Actually it's worth noting that if you are planning eating at the Saracens Head that the road down to it is very very narrow and winding (follow the signs for Symonds Yat East, unless you're towing a caravan as that definitely won't end well). You'd be much better off parking your car at the rock and walking down to it (check what time the gates are closed at Symonds Yat though!). There's limited car parking by the Inn and it's pay and display (£1.50 for up to 4 hours). You can park further down and walk back to the pub - this is also pay and display and there are signs up about clamping so make sure you have change on you.

The way back is signposted and it's a steep climb.

Clearwell Caves Coleford

Near Coleford, Royal Forest of Dean, Gloucestershire. GL16 8JR

Telephone: 01594 832535

Website: www.clearwellcaves.com

Open from March to October (please check the website as there are also special event openings).

This is an extensive natural cave system which has seen filming of both Merlin and Dr Who. Although dogs are not allowed underground there are surface walks around Clearwell Common and the lovely Clearwell Village. Parking is free (and there is plenty of it).

Offas Dyke

As far as mounds of soil go, Gloucestershire has its fair share of long barrows and forts. None is as impressive as Offas Dyke, which is basically The King of Mercia's own massive sandcastle barrier separating England from Wales, but with slightly less chance of it getting kicked over by a big boy.

15

Kingfisher cruises

Symonds Yat East, Ross-on-Wye, Herefordshire. HR9 6BL

Telephone: 01600 891063

Website: www.wyenot.com/kingfisher01.htm

The Kingfisher Cruises set off from the Saracen's Head Inn, (A Skateboard approved dog friendly pub) and are dog friendly. The cruises run several times a day from March to October.

The Dog and Muffler

Joyford, Berry Hill, Nr Coleford, Gloucestershire. GL16 7AS

Telephone: 01594 832444

Website: www.dogandmuffler.co.uk

Traditional pub grub menu from this former cider house, with mains around the £10 mark in the evenings and a selection of sandwiches and platters at lunch. Dogs allowed in the small bar.

Food served 12pm - 2:30pm and 6pm - 9:30pm. Closed Mondays unless it's a bank holiday.

Wyndham Arms Hotel

Clearwell, Near Coleford, Gloucestershire. GL16 8JT

Telephone: 01594 833666

Website: www.thewyndhamhotel.co.uk

Gastro style menu, (using meat from their own Gloucester Old Spot pigs) with mains around the £15 mark.

Food served 12pm - 2pm (2.30pm on Sunday) and 6.30pm - 9pm.

Places to eat near walks

Beechenhurst Lodge & The Speech House Hotel

Coleford, Gloucestershire. GL16 7EL

Telephone: 01594 822607

Website: www.thespeechhouse.co.uk

Twitter: @speechhouse

Former Charles II Hunting Lodge. Set in the heart of Royal Forest of Dean. Dogs are welcomed in the Orangery and the Garden. Mains at around the £10 mark. Also serve coffees and afternoon tea.

Food served from 12pm - 9pm.

Circular walk to Symonds Yat & The Saracens Head Inn

The walk can be downloaded from the Forest of Dean and Wye Valley Website here: www.ftg.org.uk/FODWVTG/12_easy_walks_wye_valley_dean.php however it's not a difficult one to follow - start at the pub - walk along one side of the river, cross the footbridge walk back on the opposite side.

Saracens Head Inn

Symonds Yat East, Ross-on-Wye, Herefordshire. HR9 6JL

Telephone: 01600 890435

Website: www.saracensheadinn.co.uk

Gastro style pub, where dogs are allowed in the bar area but not the restaurant (the bar is the one with the red telephone box in there). You might have to wait for a seat, as it gets full quickly at weekends. Gastro style menu, with mains around the £15 mark, but also a good selection of light bites and snacks for under £10.

There's covered seating outside if you can't get inside. Games cupboard with a few bits and bobs in it and a selection of newspapers. If you need to cross the river then you need to ask at the bar, and one of the staff will take you over on the pull ferry (there is a small charge for this).

Lunch served from 12pm - 2:30pm. Dinner served from 6:30pm - 9pm.

Symonds Yat Rock & The White Horse

Coleford, Gloucestershire. GL16 7NY

Telephone: 01594 833057

Website: www.forestry.gov.uk

There are a number of trails leading from the car park, or follow the easy access path to take you through the Iron Age Fort to the top of Yat Rock, one of the most stunning views in England. The log cabin serves hot and cold snacks, or poddle along to the White Horse in Staunton.

The White Horse Inn

The Conifers, Staunton Coleford, Gloucestershire. GL16 8PA

Telephone: 01594 834001

Website: www.whitehorsestaunton.co.uk

Starters and lighter bites menu hovers around the £6 mark. Main courses start at around £10 for the pie of the day and go up to the £16 mark.

Food served Tuesday - Sunday 12pm - 2:30pm and 6:30pm - 9pm. Closed on Mondays.

Things to do in Lydney

Mallards Pike Lake

Mallards Pike Lake, Park End, Lydney, Gloucestershire. GL15 4HD

How to find it: From the A48 at Blakeney take the Nibley to Parkend road. Mallards Pike is signposted on the right hand side after approximately three miles.

Mallards Pike lake is actually two lakes. The top lake is a nature reserve and the lower lake is designed for leisure activities. There's an accessible lake-side path and a sign-posted doggy dip area. Three walking trails, a way-marked family cycle route and Go Ape for the kids. Blakeney is the nearest town or village.

Go Ape

Mallards Pike Lake, Park End, Lydney, Gloucestershire. GL15 4HD

Telephone: 0845 6439215

Website: www.goape.co.uk/sites/forest-of-dean

Open weekends only in Febuary, March and November

Every day April - October. Closed December and January. Dogs are welcome.

Wilderness Discovery

Telephone: 01291 628801

Website: www.wildernessdiscovery.co.uk

Twitter: @wildwits

Contact: Alan & Karen Cree

A selection of bushcraft experiences from 2.5 hours taster sessions, to a full day tracking or foraging. Dogs welcome - as Alan pointed out, sometimes seeing how a dog reacts gives us a different perspective.

Lydney Park Estate

Lydney Park, Lydney, Gloucestershire. GL15 6BU

Website: www.lydneyparkestate.co.uk

Part of the National Gardens Scheme - formal and woodland gardens.

Sunday 8th April 2012 (Easter Sunday) through to Wednesday 6th June 2012. Open Sundays, Wednesdays and Bank Holiday Mondays.

Nagshead Bird reserve

How to find it: Take the B4234 out of Lydney towards Parkend.

Telephone: 01594 562852

Website: www.rspb.org.uk/reserves/guide/n/nagshead/about.aspx

Two way-marked nature trails (one short and one long). The visitor centre is open weekends from 10am - 4pm from the 31st of March to the end of August.

Dogs are allowed on footpaths on leads.

Explore Lydney Harbour

Harbour Road, Lydney, Gloucestershire, GL15 5ET

Recently restored.

Taurus Crafts

The Old Park, Lydney, Gloucestershire. GL15 6BU

Telephone: 01594 844 841

Website: www.tauruscrafts.co.uk

Twitter: @tauruscrafts

15 Artisan Businesses including pottery, art, food and textiles. Although dogs are not allowed in the buildings, they are allowed on site. One for a warm day when you can sit outside.

Westbury Court Gardens (see Gloucester)

Dean Forest Railway

Forest Road, Lydney, Gloucestershire. GL15 4ET

Telephone: 01594 845840

Website: www.deanforestrailway.co.uk

How to find it: On arriving in Lydney you'll find the Dean Forest Railway just off the B4234 to Whitecroft and Parkend. Follow the wooded road for about a mile and a half and you'll find the large free car park on your left.

The Railway mainly runs at weekends, with some mid-week services - check their website or check the 24 hour recorded information line on 01594 843423.

Dogs are welcome on the trains, but not on the Santa Specials or days out with Thomas (unless of course they are assistance dogs). They must be kept on a lead and off the seats.

The Miners Arms Freehouse

The Bay, Whitecroft, Gloucestershire. GL15 4PE

Telephone: 01594 562483

Website: www.minersarmswhitecroft.com

Live music most weekends including open mic nights.

Gastro style menu, with mains starting at the £10 mark.

Food served 12pm - 2:30pm and 6pm - 8:30pm.

The George Inn

High Street, Aylburton, Lydney, Gloucestershire. GL15 6DE

Telephone: 01594 842163

Website: www.millingbrooklodge.com

The George Inn also offers accommodation in the Millingbrook Lodges. Excellent value for money traditional pub menu, with mains starting at £7.

The George is open all day for drinks.

Food served Monday – Thursday 12pm - 3:30pm, and 5pm - 9pm. Friday and Saturday 12pm - 9:30pm.

Sunday carvery 12pm - 3:30pm and in the evening the normal menu 5pm - 8pm.

The Rising Sun

Moseley Green, Parkend, Lydney, Gloucestershire. GL15 4HN

Telephone: 01594 562008

Website: www.therisingsuninn-moseleygreen.co.uk

Classic pub style menu, with a good selection of light bites.

Food served Monday to Friday 12pm - 2:30pm and 6:30pm - 9:30pm. Saturday and Sunday 12pm - 2:30pm and 6:30pm - 9:30pm.

The Bailey Inn

Bailey Hill, Yorkley, Gloucestershire. GL15 4RP

Telephone: 01594 562670

Website: www.baileyinn.webs.com

Classic pub style menu, with mains starting around the £10 mark.

Food served Tuesday - Thursday 12pm - 2pm and 7pm - 9pm. Friday 7pm - 9:30pm. Saturday 4pm - 9:30pm. Sunday 12pm - 5pm. Closed Monday.

Places to eat near walks

The Fountain Inn

Fountain Way, Parkend, Nr. Lydney, Gloucestershire. GL15 4JD

Telephone: 01594 562189

Website: www.fountaininnandlodge.co.uk

Apparently (we haven't tried this) the Dean Forest railway brings you 'almost to the door' of the Fountain Inn, and they are minutes away from the Nagshead nature reserve (which has two way-marked trails). From the nature reserve go back down the drive to the entrance and walk into Parkend (there's no pavement for part of it). Traditional pub grub, along with a range of curries, with sandwiches and light snacks.

Food served all day.

The White Hart

Broadoak, Newnham on Severn, Gloucestershire. GL14 1JB

Telephone: 01594 516319

Website: www.thewhitehartbroadoak.co.uk

Slap bang on the banks of the River Severn, there's a lighter lunch menu, with good value traditional pub grub (prices around the £6 mark) or the evening menu which is also excellent value for money.

Food served 12pm - 9pm.

The Ostrich Inn

Newland, Gloucestershire. GL16 8NP

Telephone: 01594 833260

Website: www.theostrichinn.com

Gastro restaurant at the higher end of the price bracket, however the bar meals look absolutely fantastic and start around the £10 mark. Dogs are not allowed in the restaurant, but owners can eat in the bar from the restaurant menu.

Food served 12pm - 2:30pm and 6:30pm - 9:30pm.

Gardening

Within weeks of Skateboard joining our family, the 'lawn' resembled a greyhound racing track. A perfect oval of mud, surrounding a patch of scrappy grass. She also loved digging.

We read all about stopping your dog digging by burying balloons which, when faced with the weight of an over enthusiastic lurcher, would pop. We tried it. She'd not experienced excitement like this since she got too big for Greg's regular 'flying dog' exercises, where she'd lie over his forearm, tongue lolling and tail wagging as he ran around the house making spitfire noises. So the balloons were less than successful. If she found one, she'd dig more to find the little bit of deflated rubber, then throw it around the garden barking at it. Over time more and more holes appeared but it was less of a problem as she was apparently filling them in when she got fed up of digging in a particular spot.

In a seemingly unrelated problem, we'd started losing things. Hairbrushes were a favourite. She'd amble downstairs, plonk herself in front of us and give us a big doggy grin, which is when we'd notice the bits of orange rubber stuck in her teeth. I'd run upstairs to try and find my hairbrush and it would be gone, no trace apart from a few grains of rubber and a broken plastic bristle.

It wasn't until we decided to have some major building work done in the garden that we discovered her stash. Hairbrushes, knickers (never the supermarket specials, always the ones that matched something) T shirts, the doggy bandana we bought for her because it looked sweet (and which she hated from day one), all found buried in various spots in the back garden...

She still digs, but she thinks she's brilliant at hiding it (see the photo on the Dog Friendly Book website) and since we got wise to our clothes being taken out into the garden for internment, she's frisked before she's let out, especially if she's just run down the stairs with her head turned away from you...

We're about to Astroturf the back garden - this should be fun.

Winchcombe, Tewkesbury & Broadway

Things to do in Tewkesbury

Explore

Just about every time we've visited Tewkesbury we've managed to do it when it's as close to freezing as it's possible to be (see also Stow in the Wold - we never seem to head there when it's warm). As a result we know a lot of dog friendly places, because there's nothing more pathetic looking than a shivering lurcher. If you have slightly more common sense, a visit on a warm day will give you ample opportunity to have a potter round the town itself and explore the specialist shops, narrow alleyways and take in some of the beautiful architecture. There's plenty of parking, which starts from £1 for 2 hours. I like Tewkesbury a lot.

Tourist Information Centre (called Out of the Hat) can be found at 100 Church St, Tewkesbury, GL20 5AB (look for the memorial on the roundabout).

Telephone: 01684 855040

Website: www.outofthehat.org.uk

Opening times: Monday- Saturday 10am - 5pm; Bank Holidays (1st April - end September) 10am - 4pm.

Winter opening times: Mondays, Tuesdays, Fridays and Saturdays from 10am - 4pm.

Not just any old TIC, Out of the Hat has 2 floors of activities and games about the history and townspeople of Tewkesbury (there is a modest admission charge for the activities but entry to the TIC on the ground floor is free). It's always worth checking their website as well for an up to date list of activities. Dogs are allowed in the ground floor TIC (so you can get advice on any local events) but the team do ask that you remember that other visitors might not be dog lovers... The team there are really helpful and you'll find leaflets and walks around Tewkesbury for sale, as well as a Tewkesbury treasure trail.

Market days are Wednesdays and Saturdays, with the Farmers Market held on the second Thursday in the month (Spring Gardens car park in the town centre).

Antique hunting at Tewkesbury Antiques Centre

Tolsey Lane, Tewkesbury, Gloucestershire. GL20 5AE

Telephone: 01684 294091

How to find it: At the roundabout with the memorial on it, stand with your back to the Abbey and look left - you'll see the A board signposting the centre - or follow the signs for the river boat trips. The centre is on your left.

There are a number of antique shops in Tewkesbury, and the Tewkesbury Antiques Centre has 18 dealers all under one roof. Dogs are welcome on a lead and under control. Friendly team and very laid back, in fact they were a lot more relaxed with Skateboard being in there than I was (either that or they had brilliant poker faces).

Tewkesbury Abbey

Church Street, Tewkesbury, Gloucestershire. GL20 5RZ

Telephone: 01684 850959

Website: www.tewkesburyabbey.org.uk

How to find it: look upwards and keep walking towards the sticking up bit.

Dogs are not allowed in the Abbey itself, but it is still possible to appreciate the beautiful architecture from the tranquil Abbey grounds. The tea shop is also well worth a visit.

Victoria Pleasure Gardens

How to find it: Opposite the Abbey gates turn down Mill Street towards the river - the gardens are on your left unless the river's flooded - in which case you're already in trouble.

Website: www.victoriapleasuregardens.org.uk

Created to celebrate the diamond jubilee of Queen Victoria in 1897, this formal garden is small but a perfect place to just sit and watch the river slide by. Wheelchair and pushchair accessible but it does flood in winter and this can make the paths a bit on the slippy side.

Watersports at Croft Farm leisure

Croft Farm Leisure & Water Park, Bredon's Hardwick, Tewkesbury, Gloucestershire. GL20 7EE

Telephone: 01684 772321 (Ext 2)

Website: www.croftfarmleisure.co.uk

How to find it: Off the B4080

Croft Farm Leisure offer windsurfing lessons, sailing lessons and kayaking lessons. Apparently canoe trips on the River Avon with dogs are popular activities for dog owners (unless of course their dog happened to be Skateboard, in which case capsizing would be a very popular activity). If you have a dog you think will tolerate canoeing without the possibility of appearing as the 'and finally' feature on the local evening news, then what are you waiting for? If you're on a family day out then it is possible to take turns on dog duty and still have a fun packed day.

Toff Milway Conderton Pottery

The Old Forge, Conderton, Nr Tewkesbury, Gloucestershire. GL20 7PP

Telephone: 01386 725387

Website: www.toffmilway.co.uk

How to find it: Follow the brown signs from A46/A435 Roundabout at the Teddington Hands.

Open Monday - Saturday 9am - 5pm.

Saltglaze pottery with a contemporary feel.

Places to eat

The Nottingham Arms

129 High Street, Tewkesbury, Gloucestershire. GL20 5JU

Telephone: 01684 276346

Website: www.thenottinghamarms.co.uk

Dogs are allowed in the front bar area. Straightforward traditional pub menu, with a Thai night on Mondays.

Quiz on Thursday nights at 8:30pm and live music most weekends.

Food served Monday - Friday 12pm - 3pm and 6pm - 8:30pm. Saturday 12pm - 8:30pm. Sunday 12pm - 3pm.

Tearooms (an effort to find you some non-pub alternatives)

There are a number of specialist cafes and tea rooms in Tewkesbury, and if you're visiting in the summer then some of them do have seating outside. If you're visiting in the rain then Costa Coffee have a covered outside seating area (95-96 High Street, Tewkesbury, GL20 5JZ - next to the fruit and veg shop).

The Teddington Hands

Evesham Road, Teddington, Tewkesbury, Gloucestershire. GL20 8NE

Telephone: 01386 725276

Website: www.teddingtonhands.com

How to find it: At the Teddington Hands Roundabout where the A46 to Evesham & A435 to Cheltenham cross.

According to the website well-behaved dogs (on leads) and owners (lead optional) are very welcome in the bar area, but not in the restaurant. Traditional favourites from the £10 mark, and a slightly more gastro menu around the £13 mark. Large beer garden and worth a trip out to visit.

Food served Monday to Saturday 12pm - 9pm and Sunday roast between 12pm and 8pm on er…Sundays…

Places to eat near walks

Tewkesbury Riverside walk & the Lower Lode Inn

Forthampton, Gloucestershire. GL19 4RE

Telephone: 01684 293224

Website: www.lowerlodeinn.co.uk

Dogs are welcome on a lead.

Fishing available from £4 a day - please make sure you have a valid license as they are checked in Gloucestershire and you don't want your tackle seized (fnar).

Start at Tewkesbury and either cross the river in town, or walk to the very end of Lower Lode Lane (on your right after the Abbey as you are leaving Tewkesbury) and get the Hippo Ferry across the Severn to the Inn, then walk back after a good lunch. On Sundays they serve a 3 meat carvery from £7.95.

Food served 6pm - 9pm and sometimes during the day depending on the season - it's best to give them a call and check.

Tewkesbury Riverside walk & The Bell Hotel

Church Street, Tewkesbury, Gloucestershire. GL20 5SA

Telephone: 01684 293293

Website: www.oldenglishinns.co.uk/tewkesbury

Good value traditional chain pub grub, and a daily specials board. Classics menu starts from around £8 for a main. We found the comfy sofas a good place to tuck ourselves out of the way. However we were quite bemused when a set of customers moved from their table near the bar to come and watch us eat. I'd taken Skateboard's coat off as we walked in as I didn't want her to overheat. The sound of the velcro made her jump, which in turn made me jump. One of the customers asked if she was a rescue. "No" I said, and then instead of the usual explanation I added (rather unwisely) "she's just an idiot", as I was feeling a bit embarrassed that everyone was by now watching us. Anyway - as we settled down, they came to keep an eye on us - presumably to check I wasn't stabbing her with my fork between mouthfuls.

Full menu available in the bar area, where dogs are allowed.

The Bell is at the top of Mill Street, which leads down to the River. Cross the bridge to join the Severn Way. Alternatively eat at the Nottingham Arms a bit further into town.

Food served 12pm - 10pm.

The Beckford Inn

The Cheltenham Road (A46), Beckford, Nr Tewkesbury, Gloucestershire. GL20 7AN

Telephone: 01386 881532

Website: www.thebeckford.com

How to find it: On your left heading towards Evesham from Tewkesbury.

Plenty of walks around the Beckford Inn. Dogs are allowed in the grounds and the bar area, where you can choose from either the restaurant menu, or simply indulge in one of their cream teas.

Food served all day.

Alderton - The Gardeners Arms

Beckford Road, Alderton, Tewkesbury, Gloucestershire. GL20 8NL

Telephone: 01242 620257

Website: www.gardenersarms.biz

How to find it: Follow signs to Alderton from the A46 or B4077

A thatched country pub close to Tally Ho dog friendly B&B. Dogs are allowed in the garden and some of the bar areas. You'll find 2 walks to download on their website here: www.gardenersarms.biz/walks.asp

Boule area, selection of pub games (including shove ha'penny table) and Friday nights sees live acoustic guitar music - which you are encouraged to join in.

Food served Monday - Saturday 12pm - 2:15pm and 5:30pm - 9pm and Sundays 12pm - 9pm. Early bird menu available Mon - Sat from 5:30pm - 6:30pm.

Things to do in Winchcombe

Winchcombe is a beautiful little town on the outskirts of Cheltenham, which owes its prosperity to the wool trade. Walkers are welcome at Winchcombe, and many of the local traders support this initiative (see the website www.winchcombewelcomeswalkers.com).

There's a large long stay car park off Back Lane and plenty of on street parking (if you're lucky).

You'll find the tourist information centre in the Town Hall (on the corner of the main street and North Street - has a big clock on it).

Walks

Call in at the Tourist Information Centre if you're after books and leaflets of walks around Winchcombe, written by North Cotswold walkers. Dogs are not allowed on the guided walks run by the Cotswold AONB Wardens, however you will find some self guided walks to download here: www.winchcombewelcomeswalkers.com/walks/self-guided_walks.asp

The Honeybourne Line

Winchcombe Station

Website: www.gwsr.com

How to find it: To join at Winchcombe, turn down North Street and follow the brown tourist signs.

(Diesel Enthusiasts) If you want to start your journey at Toddington, then head out of Winchcombe on the B4632 towards Broadway - turn right at the roundabout and GWSR is on your right by the Pheasant Inn. You'll need to check the website for the days they're open as it varies throughout the year.

You can enjoy the Honeybourne line starting at any of its three stations - Steam train enthusiasts may opt for the journey to Cheltenham from Winchcombe. Diesel enthusiasts will want to do the Toddington route. There is a buffet car on the steam train and a 1950's style coffee shop at Winchcombe. There are dog friendly eating places in Winchcombe and Toddington (see below) If you download walk number 7 www.winchcombewelcomeswalkers.com/documents/Toddington_Circular_Walk.pdf then there is the option of returning to Winchcombe on the GWSR

When alighting at Winchcombe, be advised to give the station master a pat down, as he usually has a stash of dog treats about his person. Do let him know you're looking for dog biscuits before frisking him, especially if like me, you have a Northern accent and a disreputable looking dog.

The station master was telling me about visiting another steam railway whilst on holiday. He was chatting with a fellow passenger, who told him that he should visit the Winchcombe railway because 'The station master always has dog biscuits in his pocket'.

Winchcombe Pottery

Broadway Road, Winchcombe, Gloucestershire. GL54 5NU

Telephone: 01242 602462

Website: www.winchcombepottery.co.uk

How to find it: Heading out of Winchcombe towards Broadway, you'll see the signs for the Winchcombe pottery on your left (turn after you've gone under the railway bridge) The pottery is on your right.

The pottery itself isn't suitable for dogs of Skateboards size (due to her tail of destruction) but if you take it in turns it's definitely worth a visit to the pottery shop, as it doesn't take long to walk round.

Belas Knapp Long Barrow

Website: www.english-heritage.org.uk/daysout/properties/belas-knap-long-barrow

How to find it: signposted from the B4077

You can also walk from Winchcombe (bear in mind there are no refreshments stops en route) with views of Sudeley Castle (Download the walk from here: www.winchcombewelcomeswalkers.com/documents/Belas_Knap_walk.pdf - walk number 5)

Hailes Abbey

Hailes, Nr Winchcombe, Cheltenham, Gloucestershire. GL54 5PB

Telephone: 01242 602398

Website: www.english-heritage.org.uk/daysout/properties/hailes-abbey/

How to find it: Off the B4632 Winchcome to Broadway Road.

This English Heritage maintained site is open from 1st April until November (Check the website if you're visiting on a Monday, as sometimes they are open bank holidays and sometimes not). Once a Cistercian Abbey it held the Holy Blood of Hails - which was rumoured to be a phial of Christ's own blood. All that remains today are the foundations and a few of the arches, however there are a number of interpretation panels and a free audio tour. Alternatively just settle down in the peaceful gardens with a picnic. There is an entrance fee, unless you are a member of the National Trust or English Heritage, however dogs are welcome if they are kept on a lead. The Cotswold Way walk to Farm-cote runs past the Abbey.

Farmcote Herbs

Winchcombe, Cheltenham, Gloucestershire. GL54 5AU

Telephone: 01242 603860

Website: www.farmcoteherbs.co.uk

How to find it: Follow the signs for Farmcote after leaving Winchcombe on Castle Street (towards Guiting Power). The approach is a very narrow lane.

Over 30 varieties of chilli for sale as well as chutneys, salsas, dips and herbs. You can also buy chilli sausages and burgers - perfect if you're self catering. The Cotswold Way walk down to Hailes Abbey (above) is very very close so you can visit both places in one day if you feel so inclined.

Open May to November: Weekends, Bank Holidays Tuesdays and Wednesdays 10am - 6pm. October - November closes at 4:30pm. Closed December - April.

Stanway House & Fountain

Stanway, Cheltenham, Gloucestershire. GL54 5PQ

Telephone: 01386 584469

Website: www.stanwayfountain.co.uk

How to find it: North of Winchcombe Off the B4077.

A beautiful Jacobean manor House on the outskirts of Cheltenham. Limited opening times for the house (June July and August Tuesdays and Thursdays 2pm - 5pm) but dogs are allowed in the gardens (must be kept on a lead).

Places to eat near walks

If you fancy a gentle circular walk to Sudeley Castle then you can download one here: www.winchcombewelcomeswalkers.com/documents/Sudeley_Castle_Circular_Walk. pdf, then reward yourself with a bite to eat in one of Winchcombe's dog friendly establishments.

The White Hart Inn

High, Street, Winchcombe, Gloucestershire. GL54 5LJ

Telephone: 01242 602359

Website: www.whitehartwinchcombe.co.uk

Part of the Hatton group of pubs and hotels. Gastro style menu, (as well as the sausage specialities) with mains starting around the £13 mark. Cotwolds Cream tea served between 3pm and 6pm daily.

Food served all day.

The Plaisterers Arms

Abbey Terrace, Winchcombe, Gloucestershire. GL54 5LL

Telephone: 01242 602358

Website: www.theplaisterersarms.co.uk

Opposite some of Winchcombe's free parking (2 hours max). Traditional pub menu, with a good range of light bites and snacks. If you turn right at the main door you'll find a snug bar with a dog water bowl by the piano. We had a brown baguette with chicken and smoked ham and it was absolutely lovely. Get there early to snaffle the very comfortable leather chesterfield sofa under the window.

Food served Monday - Friday 12pm - 2:30pm and 6pm - 9pm. Saturday and Sunday 12pm - 3pm and 6pm - 9pm.

The Corner Cupboard

83 Gloucester Street, Winchcombe, Gloucestershire. GL54 5LX

Telephone: 01242 602303

Website: www.cornercupboardwinchcombe.co.uk

Good selection of baguettes and jacket potatoes on the lunchtime menu, as well as a traditional pub menu.

Food served Monday - Sunday 10am - 3pm and 6pm - 10pm.

The Pheasant Inn

Toddington Near Winchcombe, Gloucestershire. GL54 5DT

Telephone: 01242 621271

Website: www.thepheasantinn-toddington.co.uk

On the outskirts of Winchcombe on the road out to Broadway and right next to the steam railway so it's the perfect spot if you fancy a bite to eat before heading back to Cheltenham or Winchcombe. Dogs are allowed in the bar and you can choose from a breakfast, lunch, baguette, main and Thai menu (with the Thai menu also being available to take away). Looks delicious as well.

Download walk number 7 www.winchcombewelcomeswalkers.com/documents/Toddington_Circular_Walk.pdf and you'll find the Pheasant Inn right by the Toddington GWSR station (on a roundabout on the B4632 Winchcombe to Broadway Road).

Food served (in one format or another) all day.

Places to eat

The Plough Inn at Ford

Temple Guiting, Cheltenham, Gloucestershire. GL54 5RU

Telephone: 01386 584215

Website: www.theploughinnatford.co.uk

How to find it: On the B4077.

Smashing food and gorgeous desserts at the Plough Inn - it's one of our regular Sunday lunch haunts but make sure you book on Sundays as it's hugely popular. There's a daily specials board and the head chef does cater for special dietary needs. Wherever possible they use free range local meat.

Food served weekdays 12pm - 2:15pm and 6pm - 9:15pm. Weekends 12pm - 9:15pm.

Royal Oak

Gretton Road, Gloucestershire. GL54 5EP

Telephone: 01242 604999

Website: www.royaloakgretton.co.uk

On the main Winchcombe to Gretton road, 1.5 miles from Winchcombe. The Royal Oak has recently been refurbished (and it looks blooming lovely as well). If you're feeling particularly sporty then you might fancy a game of tennis as there's a court at the end of the garden. Light lunchtime options start around the £7 mark (and you can choose doorstops or thinly sliced sandwiches). Also a more substantial gastro style menu, with mains hovering around the £14 mark.

Food served 12pm - 2:30pm and 6pm - 9:30pm. Sunday lunch served 12pm - 3pm.

Things to do in Broadway

Explore Broadway itself - it really is a beautifully picturesque village. Friends of ours used to live here and were used to, although not thrilled by, people taking photographs of their living room through the stable door if it was left ajar in summer.

Broadway Tower (Also a circular walk from Broadway)

Middle Hill, Broadway, Worcestershire. WR12 7LB

Telephone: 01386 852 390

Website: www.broadwaytower.co.uk

Although dogs are not allowed in the tower, the lovely tea rooms are so dog friendly that it's no hardship to settle down with your dog whilst the rest of the family explore the tower and take in the views. The food is good value and tasty (just what you need if you've done the walk from Broadway up to the tower). Dogs usually get their own biscuits! I'm fairly sure that this was the first place we visited in the Cotswolds where not only were they happy for Skateboard to come in and say hello, she was positively welcomed.

At the time of writing it's having a bit of an overhaul, but is due to reopen in April 2012. It is under new management so we will check the dog friendly status again as soon as possible. The previous owners often had a marquee out the front so hopefully even if the status has changed you can still sit outside under cover.

Cotswold Lavender (used to be Snowshill Lavender)

Hill Barn Farm, Snowshill, Broadway, Worcestershire. WR12 7JY

Telephone: 01386 854821

Website: www.snowshill-lavender.co.uk

As well as fields of lavender to explore you'll find a tea rooms and giftshop at Cotswold Lavender - which is very dog friendly. Visitors are free to walk their dogs around the lavender fields (dogs must be kept on a lead at all times) and there are benches outside where visitors can eat and drink with their dogs (Only assistance dogs are allowed in the tearooms). Water bowls are left outside. Open March - October. It's always worth a visit, however the lavender looks at its best in June and July.

Places to eat near walks

Broadway Tower Tea Rooms

Middle Hill, Broadway, Worcestershire. WR12 7LB

As you pull into the car park for Broadway Tower you'll see a barn on your right (sometimes with an outside awning up). This is the Broadway Tower tea rooms, the perfect mid point pit stop.

Download walk www.nationaltrail.co.uk/Cotswold/uploads/walk%202%20Broadway%20revised.190210.pdf

Places to eat

The Crown Hotel Blockley (See North Cotswolds)

Crown & Trumpet

Church Street, Broadway, Worcestershire. WR12 7AE

Telephone: 01386 853202

Website: www.cotswoldholidays.co.uk

Really good traditional pub menu, with mains starting around £9. Regular Jazz & Blues live music nights and check out their website to see when the Morris Men will be appearing. Really friendly landlord here - it's been great chatting to him about the pub and accommodation.

Food served Monday - Friday 12pm - 2pm and 6pm - 9pm. Saturdays and Sundays 12pm - 9pm.

Horse & Hound Inn

54 High Street, Broadway, Worcestershire. WR12 7DT

Telephone: 01386 852287

Website: www.horse-and-hound.co.uk

Home cooked meals - 2 courses from £12.95. Dogs welcome in the bar.

Food served Monday to Friday 12pm - 3pm and 6pm - 9pm. Saturday 12pm - 3pm and 6pm - 9pm. Sunday 12pm - 3pm.

Poo

When The Boy decided to move to London, the first thing he did was to make sure all the stuff he didn't want to throw away, but didn't want to get rid of, was shipped back here. Then he asked us to drive the stuff he did want to London. We agreed as we were keen to see his new place and meet his new flat mates.

On the Friday he was due to leave (after a rousing send off from his ex-colleagues) I had scraped him out of bed and pointed him towards the coach, handing him a packed lunch that included a banana.

"You are a rubbish mum." he said "How can you forget that I hate bananas?"

"Shut up" I replied, "the potassium will help with your hangover"

The next day we put the rest of his things in the car, loaded the dog up, and set off for London.

Less than 10 minutes from the boy's new flat, Skatie stood up and started to whine. Foolishly I thought it was because she knew we were nearly there. When we were less than a minute away, her back end exploded. As the smell engulfed the car, Greg looked straight ahead

"My car" he said "my poor car".

We pulled up and all three of us spilled from the car as fast as we could. Skateboard was unable to stop the flow, all we could do was hug her and tell her it was ok and she wasn't in trouble, whilst trying to avoid the noxious liquid that was still pouring out of her and splashing on the pavement. Greg was sent to a convenience store to get antibacterial hand gel, water (to wash the pavement) J-cloths and bin bags.

We phoned The Boy, who came to meet us. Skateboard watched a seemingly familiar shape walk towards her in a totally unfamiliar place. Gradually she realised she knew exactly who that shape belonged to and began to wag her tail, adding 'knee height' to the coverage that, until that point, had been limited to her, the pavement, our shoes, ankles, cuffs and most of the back seat of the car. We washed the pavement and dabbed ineffectually at the car seats. Then we met the boy's new flat mates for the first time, both covered in liquid dog poo. Skateboard by this time felt much better, and promptly fell asleep. We drove the 100 miles home staring ahead in silence and disbelief, with the windows open and the motorway battering our ear drums.

A few weeks later, I had a meeting not far from The Boy's new place, so I popped in to see him and check how he was settling in.

"How many sugars?" he asked as he made me a cuppa.

"You are a rubbish son" I said "I don't take sugar"

Cheltenham

The 'capital' of the Cotswolds, Cheltenham became a popular health holiday destination after the discovery of Spa water in 1716. It's the home of the Cheltenham Steeplechase festival and hosts a number of cultural festivals throughout the year covering music, science, food and literature. For a full list visit www.cheltenhamfestivals.com

If you like a spot of shopping, then Cheltenham has a plethora of independent shops, as well as the larger chains dotted along the High Street. Start on the promenade at Andrew Scott jewellers (who allow well behaved dogs in the shop), then walk up the promenade towards Montpellier gardens. Some of the shops will allow dogs but best to ask first as it can vary depending on who is 'on duty'. Throughout the year various markets pop up on the Promenade at weekends - there's usually at lease one crepe stall - Skateboard rates the ham and cheese ones very highly, and always keeps her eyes peeled for children dropping theirs. If it's absolutely chucking it down then there is a reasonable amount of shelter throughout the town and enough dog friendly shops not to make it too miserable.

If you fancy a potter round the Suffolks (at the top of Montpellier) you'll find antique shops, interiors shops, boutiques and artist jewellers. Keep walking towards the Bath Road to find yet more specialist shops.

You'll find the Tourist Information Centre on the Promenade, just behind the War Memorial.

Cheltenham is ideally placed for days out further afield - you can get to Burford in under an hour, so it's the perfect place to use as a base to explore the whole of this beautiful county. For other things to do around Cheltenham, check out Gloucester, Winchcombe, Cranham and Painswick as they are under half an hour away.

Things to do in Cheltenham

Treasure Trails

Buy your treasure hunt pack for £5 from the Tourist Information Centre and follow the clues. All the answers are located on the buildings and monuments so it's a great way to explore the area. When you've finished you can submit your answer online to be entered into a prize draw. There are two Cheltenham Treasure Hunts - one for Montpellier and one exploring Pittville park.

Walking Tour

You can also buy two Audio walking tours for your iPod or other compatible device from the tourist tracks website here: www.tourist-tracks.com/tours/cheltenham.html

The Honeybourne Line

How to find it: Follow the signs to the racecourse, go in to the main entrance and follow the signs for the railway.

Website: www.gwsr.com

Train enthusiasts will want to visit the Gloucestershire Warwickshire railway, where you can take either a steam train between Cheltenham and Winchcombe or diesel round trip to Toddington. Well behaved dogs travel free (it doesn't say what they charge for badly behaved dogs). There's a buffet car on the steam train and a 1950's style coffee shop at Winchcombe. The walk into Winchcombe is only 2/3rds of a mile so why not take the early train and then explore the village? There is plenty of free parking at Cheltenham Racecourse and the railway is signposted from the main entrance. Check their website for opening times as they vary throughout the year.

Station master at Winchcombe usually has dog biscuits in his pockets.

Pittville Park

How to find it: Follow the brown heritage signs to the Pittville pump rooms - there's free parking next to and behind the pump rooms, or on road parking around the park. From Cheltenham Town centre on foot: From the High street, walk up Pittville Street (between Clarks Shoe shop and H Samuel) Keep going straight until you see the park on your right.

There are two lakes and a children's playground as well as a cage full of birds and small furries. Some areas of the park are out of bounds to dogs (including, unsurprisingly, the bit with the animals). During the holiday season, boats are available to hire on the bottom lake and if you fancy the world's longest game of pitch and putt (depending on whether or not your four legged friend is likely to fetch the ball every time you hit it) then you can hire clubs from the office by the boating lake. There is also fishing (subject to you having a valid licence).

This is a Skateboard approved park - she loves tearing onto the unoccupied fishing stations and peering into the water to see if she can see any of the lazy carp that often come up to the surface. There's also a treasure trail that features the park if you fancy playing detective. If you do decide to have a day fishing then our favourite fishing tackle shop (with resident dog) is Be Lucky Angling, 34 Edinburgh Place, Cheltenham, Gloucestershire. GL51 7SA. Telephone: 01242 575174. Website: www.beluckyangling.co.uk

Crickley Hill Country Park

How to find it: Just off the A417 between Gloucester and Cheltenham. Signposted from the B4070

The park is open every day, with a visitor centre manned from the 1st of April until the 30th of September where you can find out more about the Country park and buy leaflets with instructions for the two 'Crickley Hill' walks - one taking you round Leckhampton, and the other around Birdlip, where you could pop in to the Royal George Hotel (see below for details) for a pit stop.

Parking is £1 for 1 hour and £3 for the full day so go on - treat yourself. There are barbecues on site as well as a dedicated picnic area where dogs have to be kept on a lead. There are also toilets and a mobility scooter available for hire. Walk wise - there are a number of circular way-marked trails, including two which are suitable for pushchairs and wheelchair users. We've found that some of the marked trails aren't that easy to follow but it's almost impossible to get lost. The views are absolutely spectacular and the beech wood in autumn is a magical place. You can look at a selection of walks on the Gloucestershire County Council website here: www.gloucestershire.gov.uk/index. cfm?articleid=1428

The nearby Air Balloon pub doesn't allow dogs inside but there is a covered seating area where you can order and eat food outside - however if you want to be inside your nearest 100% dog friendly pub would be the Royal George Hotel in Birdlip (Which you'll find listed in the Gloucester section)

Places to Eat

The Montpellier Chapter

Bayshill Road, Montpellier, Cheltenham. GL50 3AS

Telephone 01242 527788

Website: www.themontpellierchapterhotel.com

As well as being a dog friendly hotel, the bar at the Montpellier Chapter is a super dog friendly eatery. With the bar food hovering around the £10 mark you can sit back and relax in gorgeous surroundings whilst watching the world go by.

Food served all day.

A nice cup of tea and a sit down (pub alternatives)

Although they don't allow dogs in the premises, there is covered seating outside John Gordons Whisky shop towards the top of Montpellier. Here you can get a decent cup of tea and lovely cake whilst sitting under cover. Many of the smaller cafes have outside seating as do the larger chains like All Bar One and Strada which you'll find at the top of Montpellier. Heading further into town (towards the Promenade) you'll find the Swallow Bakery which also has covered outdoor seating. They do a superb sausage lattice - Skateboard thoroughly approves, as it's quite crumbly pastry and she's very enthusiastic about clearing anything that drops from your hand...

The Kemble Brewery Inn

27 Fairview St, Cheltenham. GL52 2JF

Telephone: 01242 243446

How to find it (on foot): off the Cheltenham ring road where Fairview Road becomes St Johns Street (Bence's builders merchants on the corner), you'll see an old Victorian school that's been converted into flats. Turn right in front of it and follow the road round.

A tiny real ale pub tucked away in a Cheltenham side street - it is difficult to find but it's worth the search - it has a range of hearty snacks and sandwiches and is very dog friendly. There's a lovely walled garden with plenty of seating and a covered area.

Tuesday night is Quiz night if you fancy your chances against the locals. Good range of hearty sandwiches and snacks.

Food serving times vary so it's best to call them in advance.

The Bayshill

85 St Georges Place, Cheltenham. GL50 3PP

Telephone: 01242 524388

Website: www.bayshillpub.com

Really friendly local pub just off the Royal Well - so perfect to pop in after a morning exploring the shops in Cheltenham. A selection of real ales, excellent value food - pub classics with daily specials. The main courses are HUGE and straightforward good value, however, there's also a good range of snacks perfect for sharing. Dogs are allowed in the bar area (the two bits at the front of the pub). There's a rear garden where dogs are also allowed. The nearest car park is the Royal Well pay & display car park, as the on-street parking fills up quickly.

Food served from 12pm - 2pm and 5:30pm - 9pm

The Beehive

1 - 3 Montpellier Villas, Cheltenham. GL50 2XE

Telephone: Bar: 01242 702270 Restaurant: 01242 579443

Website: www.thebeehivemontpellier.com

Twitter: @TheBeehivechelt

If you've discovered the Suffolks and Tivoli, then you'll know that you can walk up quite an appetite exploring the fantastic range of shops, just a few minutes away from the main town centre. We suggest (and Skateboard heartily agrees) a visit to the Beehive in Montpellier. If we lived a little closer then this would be our regular haunt. The garlic mushrooms on toast with stilton are delicious.

The first time we ventured there, and after I'd been served, we were asked straight away if Skateboard needed water - which I was really impressed with. Have a look at the nooks and crannies (You'll find jigsaws etc near the fireplace). Plenty of places to tuck yourself away for an afternoon with the papers. Highly recommended. If you're doing the Montpellier Tourist tracks walk, The Beehive is on your right between point 8 and point 9.

Food served Monday to Saturday 12pm - 2:30pm and 6pm - 9pm. Sunday 12pm - 3pm.

The Swan

37 High Street, Cheltenham. GL50 1DX

Telephone: 01242 243726

Website: www.theswancheltenham.co.uk

Just opposite the entrance to Sandford Park is the Swan - a dog friendly pub with a lovely covered outside terrace (although dogs are allowed inside on a lead). There are lovely squashy leather sofas at the front and because the bar is long and thin with lots of little alcoves it is possible to tuck yourselves away. Monday night is the extremely popular quiz night. Food wise, The Swan provides reasonably priced pub grub (sausages and mash being a speciality). If you're staying at either Badger Towers, Charlton Kings Hotel or the Cotswold Grange Hotel and you've had a shopping day then this is en route back to your accommodation - give the dog a good run on Sandford Park, then settle down for some food before heading back.

Food served Monday - Thursday 12pm - 2pm and 5pm - 9pm. Friday, Saturday and Sunday 12pm - 9pm.

The Strand

40-42 High Street, Cheltenham. GL50 1EE

Telephone: 01242 511848

Website: www.strandpub.co.uk

Twitter: @strandpub

Laid back gastro style pub opposite The Swan, so same applies re distance from accommodation. Really good value lunchtime offers (ham, egg and chips for £5.50 - yes please). Regular events including gourmet burger nights, televised live rugby and regular music nights. One of The Boy's regular haunts when he's back in Cheltenham.

Food served Monday to Friday 12pm - 2.30pm and 6pm - 9pm. Saturday 12pm - 8pm. Sunday 12pm - 4pm.

The Royal Well Tavern

5 Royal Well Place, Cheltenham. GL50 3DN

Telephone: 01242 221212

Website: www.theroyalwelltavern.com

Twitter: @tavernchelt

Brought to you by the same team behind the Wheatsheaf in Northleach, the Royal Well Tavern has just been refurbished. Gastro style menu, with plates around the £8 mark and daily specials around £15.

Food served from 9am until late 7 days a week.

Places to eat near walks

The Rising Sun Hotel

Cleeve Hill, Cheltenham, Gloucestershire. GL52 3PX

Telephone: 01242 676281

Website: www.oldenglishinns.co.uk/cheltenham/

Dogs are welcome in the Rising Sun - and they have a record for being extremely child friendly as well (children have their own child size cutlery - why don't more places think of this?) Offering absolutely spectacular views of Cheltenham, a walk on Cleeve Hill will get your appetite going - please make sure that you follow the instructions when you are on Cleeve as there are often sheep grazing. Download walk number 5 from www.nationaltrail.co.uk/cotswold/text.asp?PageId=54 Cleeve Hill Common Ring - you can either do the 4 mile or the 6 mile version. As you are finishing the walk (having passed the masts) look out for Rising Sun Lane on your left, follow it and you'll come out at the Rising Sun pub.

Food served all day.

The Plough

Mill Street, Prestbury, Cheltenham. GL52 3BG.

Telephone: 01242 222180

Website: www.ploughprestbury.co.uk

Twitter: @ploughprestbury

Prestbury is a little way out of Cheltenham, towards Winchcombe on the B4632. It's reported to be one of the most haunted villages in the UK with a White Lady, a Headless Horseman and a Black Abbott (The Black Abbott now only appears in the churchyard since the Church was exorcised). It's reported that the sound of hooves can be heard at the Plough Inn.

Steel your nerves with a traditional pub menu - good value mains starting at around £8. Nice selection of sandwiches and sides as well. The Plough isn't too far from Cleeve Hill either, so also handy for walks.

Food served Monday to Saturday 12pm - 2:30pm and 6pm - 9pm. Sunday lunch 12pm - 6pm.

Partridges

After Skateboard's exploding back end incident we had to get the car thoroughly valeted and steam cleaned. It was a hell of a job, and when we finally got the car back the seats were still a little damp.

Not wanting to leave the windows open overnight, we decided to embrace our inner pensioner and 'go for a bit of a run out' with the windows open, to try and get the car a bit drier. The sun was starting to go down so I grabbed my camera and we set off up Cleeve Hill to try and catch the sunset. About 50 pictures later I finally had one I didn't think was rubbish... and the car seats were still wet.

We decided to push on towards Winchcombe via Belas Knap. We'd just gone through Charlton Abbots, when up ahead of us we found the road blocked by what looked like a running club. A running club for partridges. About 30 of them running up the hill in front of us. We slowed right down, expecting them to scatter but they totally ignored us and continued up the hill, with us trundling along behind them at about 5 mph. But there were partridges!

"Look at the partridges!" I'm pretty sure I was clapping and squealing with glee at one point. I'm 44.

Cute as they were, we really needed to get the car seats dry. We hatched (sorry) a plan. Greg stopped and let me out, I shooed the partridges out of the road and he drove past them, then accelerated about 30 yards up the road.

After my initial suspicion he was going to leave me, I realised he was just putting some space between us and the covey of birds. I started to walk towards the car. So did the partridges. I walked quicker. So did the partridges. I broke into a run... they took off and flew. By the time I reached the passenger door there were once again 30 partridges standing in front of the car, squinting at me through the headlights. And of course, the minute Greg began to inch the car forwards they turned their backs and ran ahead of us.

We repeated this twice more, out of the car, shoo the birds, race the birds, fail. Greg by this time was laughing like a drain, and I was starting to mutter about 'pies' under my breath. I'd finally been allowed back in the car to recover after three woman v partridge uphill races, and we were just in the middle of the 'but what will we do if we squish one of them?' discussion, when without warning they all veered off to the left and we were free to pass.

The seats still weren't dry by the time we got home.

Gloucester

Covers:

Birdlip

Gloucester

Longhope

Upton St Leonards

Slimbridge/Frampton & Arlingham

Sadly Gloucester City Council don't seem to have Dog Friendly on their radar for Gloucester itself. The new quayside Designer Outlet for example is as dog unfriendly as it's possible to get (dogs are not even allowed in the open air parts), and as the Antiques centre has now moved into the designer outlet they are no longer allowed to let dogs in (which they used to do). The designer outlet itself still isn't 100% occupied and frankly if you're on holiday then I'd suggest you shop in your home town.

Explore the Gloucester Quays

Although the shopping part of the Quays (above) isn't remotely dog friendly I still enjoy a potter down to the Quays. There is covered seating if it's raining and the family want to venture into the museums or shopping centre. There's also covered outside seating at Coots cafe (next to the Waterways Museum).

Take a boat trip from the Waterways Museum

Llanthony Warehouse, The Docks, Gloucester. GL1 2EH

Telephone: 01452 318200

Website: www.gloucesterwaterwaysmuseum.org.uk

Dogs are allowed on the daily 45 minute boat trips on the Queen Boadicea between April and October, but they're not allowed on the scheduled cruises. Tickets are available from the Waterways Museum. Sailing Midday, 1:30pm and 2:30pm. Adults £4.95, Children £3.50.

Gloucester Cathedral

Of course, dogs are not allowed in the Cathedral, but the outside of it is absolutely stunning and worth a walk around.

Robinswood Hill Country Park & Rare Breeds Centre

Reservoir Road, Gloucester. GL4 6SX

Telephone: 01452 304779

Free car parking and visitor centre. A number of way-marked trails and top of our visit list.

St James City Farm

23 Albany Street, Tredworth, Gloucester. GL1 4NG

Telephone: 01452 305728

Website: www.stjamescityfarm.co.uk

Run as a community project, the Gloucester City Farm has cows, sheep, pigs, goats and small furries as well as running a number of projects teaching young people about agriculture and farming. Free entry.

Monday to Saturday 9:30am to 4:30pm. Dogs must be kept on a lead.

Gloucester Ghost Walks

Website: www.gloucesterghostwalks.co.uk

How about taking your pooch for a bit of moral support on one of Gloucester's popular Ghost Walks. You can book a walk on Wednesday or Thursday nights starting out from outside the Gloucester Tourist Information Centre on Southgate Street. Lynn (who runs the walks) has suggested that you check which route they are doing in advance, as a few places prefer the dogs to be kept outside but "thankfully not many". Up to date prices and contact details are on the website on the booking page.

Make sure to practice your Scooby Doo and Shaggy impressions before you go.

Treasure trails

If you have children as well as dogs then there are two treasure trails in Gloucester they will enjoy (Blood hound owners MAY have an advantage). One of the trails covers Gloucester heritage and the second looks at the city and the historic docks.

Lassington Woods

How to find it: East of Highnam and is well signposted from Oakridge, off the B4215 north of Gloucester.

Parking is in a lay-by at the entrance to the woods.

Walks around a network of footpaths. There's a huge hollow trunk in the centre of the wood, which is the last of the 'Lassington Oak'.

Westbury Court Gardens

Westbury-on-Severn, Gloucestershire. GL14 1PD

Telephone: 01452 760461

Website: www.nationaltrust.org.uk/westburycourt

How to find it: On the A48 between Gloucester and Lydney. Signposting isn't brilliant, so keep your eyes peeled.

Dutch style water garden with canals and clipped hedges. Dogs welcome on a short lead. National Trust Property. Usually closed Mondays and Tuesdays, although open all week during July and August from 10am - 5pm.

Places to eat

Seriously? Come on Gloucester sort it out!

Places to eat near walks (but apparently not in Gloucester)

The Hawbridge Inn

Haw Bridge, Tirley, Gloucestershire. GL19 4HJ

Telephone: 01452 780316

Website: www.hawbridgeinn.co.uk

After a bracing walk along the river, then the Hawbridge Inn is perfect for refueling. Good value daily offers and an extensive sausage menu, where you can choose from a range of sausages and pick your mash from a selection of 7 different sorts and 4 different types of gravy or sauce. Prices start from £7 for traditional sausages and £9 for speciality. Also has a traditional lunch menu, with prices starting around the £8 mark.

Food served 12pm - 2:30pm and 6pm - 9pm except Tuesdays and Sundays.

The Royal George Hotel

Birdlip, Gloucestershire. GL4 8JH.

Telephone: 01452 862506

Website: www.oldenglishinns.co.uk/birdlip

You can buy the walk directions from the visitor centre at Crickley Country Park (see Cheltenham) or download from the website here: www.gloucestershire.gov.uk/utilities/action/act_download.cfm?mediaid=35172 It's around 5 miles and should take you about 2 hours. Although it is way-marked we have found that it is possible to get lost, so it's worth making sure that you do have the leaflet with you. At point 7 on the map you have the option of doing a quick detour into Birdlip village where you'll find the Royal George Hotel. It does get very busy at weekends and although it is welcoming we tend to head somewhere a bit quieter due to Skateboard's 'particular' disposition. Meals however are good - mains start from the £9 mark and if you fancy a lighter bite then the sharing platters are good, alternatively the lighter bites menu is available until 5pm.

Food served all day.

Fostons Ash

Slad Road, The Camp, Nr Birdlip, Gloucestershire. GL6 7ES

Telephone: 01452 863262

Website: www.food-club.com/fostons-ash.htm

Again a gastro style menu, with mains starting at the £11.00 mark. Part of the Food Club brand (and we love the Old Fleece so this should also be good).

Food served 11am - 2:45pm and 6pm - 10pm weekdays and Saturdays, 11am - 10pm Sundays.

Things to do around Slimbridge

Canal Visitor Centre at Saul

The Canal Towpath, Church Lane, Saul, Gloucestershire. GL2 7LA.

Telephone: 07854 026 504

Website: www.cotswoldcanals.com/pages/visitor-centres/saul.php

Open on Saturdays and Sundays throughout the year.

Not brilliantly signposted. When you've crossed the river on the B4071 at Frampton follow the road round to the right. Entering Saul you'll find the church on your right, turn right down Church Lane and follow the road round. The Visitor centre car park is on your left before you go to cross the river again.

Opening Hours: Saturday 12:30pm - 4pm Sunday 12:30pm - 4pm Dogs are allowed in the visitor centre (one at a time strictly) and on Sundays they do 20 minute trips on the canal. Parking is £1 for 4 hours. Good walks either way along the tow path. Visitor centre has 'dog mooring point' to the left (don't worry - it's on land).

The Stables Cafe at Saul Junction

Sandfield Bridge, Canal Bank, Saul, Gloucestershire. GL2 7LA

Telephone: 01452 741965

Website: www.thestablescafe.co.uk

Right next to the Saul Canal Visitor centre and immediately on your left before the car park - with both open and covered seating. Opening hours vary month on month depending on the season so best to check the website, although generally open between 10am and 4:30pm daily.

The Severn Bore

Nope - not the old chap sitting in the corner with a pint and a burning desire to tell you his views on the European monetary system, but a weird tidal wave that travels up the river, and is often ridden by surfers. If you're visiting Gloucestershire at the right time of year, then check out the Severn bore timetable at www.severn-bore.co.uk.

Places to eat near walks

The Ship Inn

Moore Street, Upper Framilode, Gloucestershire. GL2 7LH

Telephone: 01452 740260

Website: www.shipinnframilode.co.uk

From the Saul Canal visitor centre turn left, then when you are opposite the junction house turn left again to follow the old canal into Framilode. Dogs are allowed in the bar area, however I have no idea what the food is like, as all three of the people behind the bar were determined not to catch my eye, so we left (sorry). I admit that I hesitated about putting this bit in - or even mentioning the pub, but decided that as there had been good reviews previously I would. Hopefully I just visited on a bad day, and you'll have a great walk and fantastic food.

Canalside walk and The Tudor Arms

Shepherds Patch Slimbridge, Gloucestershire. GL2 7BP

Website: www.thetudorarms.co.uk

Telephone: 01453 890306

Right next to the Gloucester-Sharpness Canal, so a good old walk to build up an appetite.

Bar meals are served all day and the restaurant menu is served between 12pm - 2pm and 6pm - 9pm daily, with mains starting at around the £10 mark.

Circular walk & The Red Lion

The High Street, Arlingham, Gloucestershire. GL2 7JN

Telephone: 01452 740700

Website: www.redlionarlingham.co.uk

Download four circular walks around Arlingham here www.community.stroud.gov. uk/_documents/22_arlinghamlflt.pdf although the leaflets are also available from the Old Passage Inn and the Red Lion.

Good value traditional (if a bit limited) pub grub, but with mains starting at £9, and the meal deals, you really can't grumble.

Food served Wednesday to Saturday 12pm - 2:30pm and 6:30pm - 8:45pm. Sunday lunch served 12:30pm - 3:30pm.

The bit where we tell people the dog's name

Jill, Clare and I had just taken Skateboard for a good walk and were approaching a kissing gate that was being manned by a girl of about 11.

"I like your dog" she said.

"Thank you" said Jill.

"What's it's name?"

"Skateboard" Jill replied. There a brief pause.

"Skateboard!!?"

It happens a lot.

Stroud & Area

Stroud district Council have put together an excellent resource with downloadable walks here:

www.strollinginstrouddistrict.org/downloadablewalks.asp

Things to do in and around Painswick, Cranham & Sheepscombe

Travelling along the A46 from Cheltenham to Stroud, you'll find the picturesque village of Painswick but don't rush here, as there are plenty of places to visit on your route (Coopers Hill, Prinknash Abbey (no dogs inside unfortunately) and Cranham).

When you do arrive however, rather than looking for parking in the centre (most of the streets only allow for one car to get through at a time and you WILL get stuck) go straight through the traffic lights (travelling towards Stroud) and past the church, where you'll find a pay & display car park on your left (with toilets and an information board). Parking is free on a Sunday but it'll hardly break the bank the rest of the week as it starts from 30p for an hour.

From the car park walk back up towards the centre of town - the Tourist Information Centre has relocated from the (now closed) library to the town hall, which you'll find opposite the top entrance to the church yard. It's open Monday - Friday. Take a few minutes to look at the arch of 99 sculpted yew trees leading you down to the entrance of the church - (in fact because the streets are so narrow if you are going to walk towards the centre then it's best to cut through the church yard).

Painswick Rococco Gardens

Gloucester Road, Painswick, Gloucestershire. GL6 6TH

Telephone: 01452 813204

Website: www.rococogarden.org.uk

Twitter: @RococoGarden

How to find it: Follow the brown tourists signs from the centre of Painswick.

A little way out of Painswick. Walkable from town, although it's a hill and there is no pavement for the last little bit of it. Entry is £6.50 although the gardens are closed from the 31st October to 10th January. Dog friendly but dogs must be kept on a lead.

Opening times: 11am - 5pm.

Art & Artists & Shopping in Painswick

There is a thriving arts community in Painswick - on the main A46 you'll find the Fiery Beacon Gallery (small dogs allowed in but best if you pick them up and don't forget that breakages have to be paid for - this is definitely NOT one for Skateboard and her table-height 'tail of doom'). If it's raining, there's a small porch to shelter in - but the Falcon is only a bit down the road so I'd be inclined to sit in there with a cream tea. In the centre of the village is the Gloucestershire Guild of Craftsmen www.guildcrafts.org. uk. Again, you can shelter in the hallway, but why would you when the Royal Oak is a stones throw away.

Walks around Painswick area

Coopers Hill Nature Reserve

This is currently one of Skateboard's favourites - she actually whines when we go past the first car park as she thinks she knows where she's going. The noise gets a little louder if we go past the second one on our way further afield.

How to find it: You'll find the Reserve on the A46 between Brockworth and Prink-nash Abbey on the way to Painswick. Travelling from Brockworth you'll see a disused/closed car park on your left then immediately after you'll find the one in use, with a nature trail signpost at the back of the parking area. Coming from Painswick, start looking for the car park on your right as soon as you've passed the Abbey on your left. There are currently no dog waste bins here so make sure you have plenty of bags.

Coopers Hill is the home of the famous Cheese Rolling - and the clue to the walk is in the name 'Hill' there's no gentle easing in to this one - it's out of the car park and start climbing. Needless to say it's not suitable for pushchairs and it's a bit dodgy with a hangover as well. There is a way-marked nature trail (follow the green arrows) which is better than some, but they're not as easy to spot once you get to the top of the woods (after you've looked down Coopers Hill and gone past the maypole) so we usually bimble about a bit until we find one of the other paths and make our way back to the car park.

You can get more information about the woods and the nature reserve and download a route of the walk and a fact sheet here: www.gloucestershire.gov.uk/index.cfm?articleid=1427

If you need refreshments and a loo break then Prinknash Abbey is a few minutes up the road and they do superb home made cakes. You can't take dogs into the Abbey coffee shop but there is nearly always a dog bowl outside, and the team who run it are happy to bring trays out. The Black Horse at Cranham is a few minutes away either by car on foot.

Places to eat near walks

For Foston's Ash see Gloucester

The Black Horse Cranham & Cranham Woods

Cranham, Gloucestershire. GL4 8HP

Telephone: 01452 812217

Closed on Mondays.

How to find it: it's en route on your walk but if you just want to go for food then follow Buckholt road into the centre of Cranham from the A46 and you'll see it on your right up the hill.

Download the national Trails walk (number 7) Cranham, Cooper's and the Beechwoods from www.nationaltrail.co.uk/cotswold/text.asp?PageId=54. The walk starts at the car park on the outskirts of Cranham (on your left - you can see the national trails sign at the back of the car park). It joins the Cotswold way for some of it then takes you up to Coopers Hill (see Coopers Hill Nature Reserve). As you pass the scout hut turn left and walk a little way up the hill until you come to a turning on your right. You'll see the pub at the top of the road.

The Black Horse offers a range of home-cooked traditional pub food and generous portions starting around £9 and the menu is really very good. The sausage and bacon toad in the hole is a winner.

Last time we ate there Skatie had managed to find something stinky to roll in so we decided (for the sake of everyone else) to eat outside. It was February, and once again we had the journey home with the windows down. Braveheart she may have been whilst out, but as soon as I took her into the bathroom she didn't look quite so cocky when she realised what was about to happen. In case you didn't know - tomato juice is very good at neutralising nasty niffs from fox or badger droppings...

There's a second (longer) downloadable walk here: www.strollinginstrouddistrict.org/downloads/CCC5.pdf which also takes you through the village of Sheepscombe where you'll find the Butchers Arms www.butchers-arms.co.uk

Don't despair if you can't download the walks, as it is possible to walk most of them without instructions, due to the excellent trail signs showing you where you are at major junctions (we have already mentioned that the signage isn't so good past Coopers Hill but follow the edge of the woods and you'll find yourself back at one of the trail signs). The other great thing about the trail signs is that you can make your walk longer or shorter (for example sometimes we just walk Buckholt wood then follow Buckholt road round before jumping back on the public footpath back down into Cranham).

Painswick Beacon & the Royal William

How to find it: On the A46 between Cheltenham and Painswick

Another Iron Age Hill Fort with astounding views. As you travel towards Painswick from Cheltenham look out for a turning on your right signposted Catbrain quarry. The road is narrow and windy and there's a few Chelsea tractors come whipping down so - y'know... Once you've passed the entrance to the quarry (and seen the signposts for the Cotswold Way and the Wysis Way), bear right. There's plenty of free parking ahead of you (cars really do crack through here as it's a rat run avoiding Painswick village centre so make sure that you keep your dog close in the car parking areas). There's a dog poo bin in the car park. For walks - take your pick! If you want to walk up to the fort (and usually the views are worth it) then head back towards the golf course from the car park and turn left. You'll see the cotswold stone paths leading up the hill and there's an information board under the fir tree on the left.

Once you've reached the top and taken in the views (or not - have a look at our picture on the Dog Friendly Book website) then walk down the 'back' of the fort and follow the footpath which will bring you out next to the Royal William Pub.

The Royal William

Cheltenham Road, Cranham, Gloucestershire. GL6 6TT

Telephone: 01452 813 650

Website: www.royalwilliam.co.uk

Dogs are allowed in the bar area and owners are welcome to choose from a selection of baguettes, lighter bites or the full menu including the 'hot rocks' - volcanic rocks which cook your meal at a very high temperature at your table. Not sure this would be a good idea with Skateboard but it looks absolutely delicious.

Food served every day from 12pm until 9pm.

Places to eat

The Royal Oak

St Mary's Street, Painswick, Gloucestershire. GL6 6QG

Telephone 01452 813129

Website: www.theroyaloakpainswick.co.uk

A traditional Cotswold pub. Dogs are allowed in the bar area (turn left at the door) and you can eat there. You might be tempted to try the Puppy Pie - this is a traditional dish with a story. Villagers from Stroud were told they had been fed pies made from stray dogs as the villagers in Painswick were too poor to buy meat. The new landlord has resurrected the dish.

Food served daily from 10am - 9pm. No real puppies used in the pies, we promise. A more traditional pub menu.

The Falcon

New Street, Painswick, Gloucestershire. GL6 6UN

Telephone: 01452 814222

Website: www.falconpainswick.co.uk

When we last visited Painswick The Falcon certainly wasn't dog friendly but the new owner David, who took over in May 2011, has made a massive difference to the atmosphere, the food, and the dog friendly status. The interior has been completely refitted (think gastro pub) and the smells from the kitchen as you open the door - wow! Mains around the £14 mark.

Food served all day starting with breakfast at 7:30am.

The Butchers Arms

Sheepscombe, Gloucestershire. GL6 7RH

Telephone: 01452 812113

Website: www.butchers-arms.co.uk

On the main road through Sheepscombe (which is very narrow) you'll find the Butchers Arms. Parking can be a bit trying at weekends (unless you have a second home in the Cotswolds and a really big car. Special rules for you mean that apparently you can park where you bally well like).

Traditional lunch menu starts from £10 or go for a light lunch at around the £6 mark.

Food served Monday - Friday 12pm - 2:30pm and 6:30pm - 9:30pm. Saturday 12pm - 9:30pm. Sunday 12pm - 8pm (6pm in January and February).

The Crown Inn

Frampton Mansell, Stroud, Gloucestershire. GL6 8JG

Telephone: 01285 760601

Website: www.thecrowninn-cotswolds.co.uk

Gastro style menu, with mains starting at around £10. Booking advised Fridays, Saturdays and Sundays.

Food served 12pm - 2:30pm and 6pm - 9pm.

The Old Badger Inn

Alkerton Road, Springhill, Eastington, Gloucestershire. GL10 3AT

Telephone: 01453 822892

Website: www.oldbadgerinn.co.uk

The Old Badger Inn recently reopened after refurbishment. We were tipped off about it by the team at the Saul Canal Visitor centre who told us that the Inn do regular guided dog walks. Speaking to the landlady, it transpires that the chap who ran them no longer lives in the area, but they are hoping to start them again very soon, so give them a ring.

Food served Tuesday - Thursday 12pm - 3pm and 6pm - 9pm. Friday and Saturday 12pm - 3pm (Main menu) and 6pm - 9pm (Tapas menu). Sunday 12pm - 3pm. Kitchen closed Mondays and Sunday evenings.

Things to do in Minchinhampton, Rodborough & Amberley

Walk of course! although this is common land so there is livestock on it.

Perfect for kite flying (unless you have a dog that runs a mile when you show her a kite), or just sitting and taking in the views. There's some great places to eat and drink so if you've forgotten your picnic then you're not going to have to leave the common in search of food.

Minchinhampton Village itself is worth an explore, with its covered market hall and church. You can do a short loop if you walk from the market place with the hall on your left up to the top of the road, turn left and walk across the common then follow the road down past the church to come back out into the market place - it's not the longest walk but Skateboard does like to have a quick burn on the common, and it's far enough away from the road for us not to worry.

WARNING - Fairly high "dog in handbag" probability in a couple of the pubs.

Places to eat near walks

The Black Horse Inn

Littleworth, Amberley, Stroud, Gloucestershire. GL5 5AL.

Telephone: 01453 872556

Website: www.blackhorseamberley.co.uk

A favourite, especially for summer evenings where the view from the back beer garden is absolutely spectacular. This is the start/end point for the Amberley Circular walk and well worth a stop. Download the Amberley Circular walk here (it's walk number 9) www.cotswoldsaonb.org.uk/userfiles/file/Walks/WalksOnWheels_WALK9.pdf. There used to be an Annual Beer & Blues festival, which saw the conservatory at the back of the pub opened up as a stage and the beer festival in a marquee at the front of the pub. Dogs welcome on a lead. They are planning more events this year and they are listed on the website.

Food served Monday - Friday 12pm - 2:30pm and 6pm - 9pm. Weekends from 12pm - 9pm.

The Bear of Rodborough

Rodborough Common, Stroud, Gloucestershire. GL5 5DE

Telephone: 01453 878522

Website: www.cotswold-inns-hotels.co.uk/property/the_bear_of_rodborough

Dogs allowed in the bar area. Gastro style dining, with mains starting at the £10 mark.

Food served 12pm - 2:30pm and 6:30pm - 10pm. Afternoon tea served from 2:30pm - 6pm

Amberley Inn

Culver Hill, Amberley, Stroud, Gloucestershire. GL5 5AF

Telephone: 01453 872565

Website: www.theamberleyinn.co.uk

After a good walk on the common, come and meet Peggy, the resident dog.

Pop in for a cream tea in the summer or something a bit more substantial. Dogs allowed in the bar areas. Trevor from the Amberley Inn was explaining that Peggy is the reason they ended up there. Originally planning to sail around the world with her owners, Peggy wasn't massively impressed at the toilet arrangements on the boat, so subsequently had to be taken ashore each time she needed to 'go'. Not quite as easy as opening the back door and putting the outside light on. Showing true devotion to their four legged friend, the plan was abandoned. Go in and buy Trevor a pint for making a difficult call (and tell him Rachael from the Dog Friendly Book sent you).

Food served every day 12pm - 3pm and 6:30pm - 9pm.

Halfway House

Box Village Nr Minchinhampton, Gloucestershire. GL6 9AE

Telephone: 01453 832 631

Website: www.thehalfwayhousebox.co.uk

Dogs are allowed in the bar area, where you can choose from either the bar menu or the a la carte menu. Classic bar menu mains start from the £10 mark with a range of sandwiches starting at £5. A La Carte menu mains around £15 either way.

Food served Tuesday to Saturday 12pm - 2:30pm and 6pm - 10pm. Sunday lunch 12pm - 4:30pm. No food on Mondays.

The Old Lodge

Minchinhampton Common, Stroud, Gloucestershire. GL6 9AQ

Telephone: 01453 832047

Website: www.food-club.com/old-lodge.htm

Twitter: @Nick_and_Chris

Gastro style menu, with mains around the £15 mark. Part of the Food Club brand.

Food served Monday - Friday 11am - 14:45pm and 6pm - 10pm. Weekends 11am -10pm.

Things to do in Nailsworth

We have a soft spot for Nailsworth. During the 'great flood of Cheltenham' back in 2007 there was no water in or around Cheltenham (unless you counted the huge pools of mud left by the river bursting its banks). The council and the army installed water bowsers (which were emptied pretty much as soon as they were filled) and we had to rely on an early morning strip wash, standing at a washing up bowl of warm water. Of course there was no way of flushing the loo, so we had everything it was possible to collect water in, spread out in the back garden to catch the rain.

For the first few days it was quite fun - the bowsers provided an opportunity for the neighbours to meet and chat and the whole street took it in turns to check that the older householders had water available. But after the initial 'fun' had worn off, we realised that we really did need some clean clothes. Neither of us like shopping, and we both have a 'do I really need this?' attitude to new 'things' (unless it's made by Apple - in which case the answer is almost always 'yes I do').

We didn't need new clothes - we needed clean clothes, so we packed all the washing into holdalls and set off in search of somewhere with a water supply. And that was when we found Nailsworth. The launderette was packed - the only option was a service wash. When we explained our predicament to the guy who owned it, he sent us off to the nearest pub for a sit down, and told us to come back in an hour and a half instead of the next day...

We had a fabulous relax, sitting with the papers outside the pub, and enjoying an afternoon bunking off work.

Places to eat

The Britannia - Nailsworth

Britannia Inn, Cossack Square, Nailsworth, Gloucestershire. GL6 0DG

Telephone: 01453 832501

Website: www.food-club.com/britannia.htm

Twitter: @Nick_and_Chris

Fantastic range of stonebaked pizzas to eat in or take away. Part of the Food Club brand who "provide drinking water, doggy bags and a smile, and never make charges for any dog related service".

Food served Monday - Friday 11am - 2:45pm and 5:30pm - 10pm. Weekends 11am - 10pm.

Tipputs Inn - Nailsworth

Bath Road, Nailsworth, Gloucestershire. GL6 0QE

Telephone: 01453 832466

Website: www.food-club.com/tipputs.htm

Twitter: @Nick_and_Chris

Choose from traditional British menu - with a bit of a twist (mains start at around £12) or Moggu South Indian cuisine. Part of the Food Club brand.

Food served Monday - Friday 11am - 2:45pm and 5:30pm - 10pm. Weekends 11am - 10pm.

The Weighbridge Inn

Longfords, Minchinhampton, Stroud, Gloucestershire. GL6 9AL

Telephone: 01453 832520

Website www.2in1pub.co.uk

Twitter: @2in1pie

How to find it: You'll find the Weighbridge Inn on the B4014 between Nailsworth and Avening.

We'd read about the famous 2 in 1 pies served at the Weighbridge Inn, so decided to go and try them for ourselves on one of our regular Sunday jaunts. Even though we didn't arrive until 2 we only just managed to get the last table - which Skateboard happily 'hurumphed' under after a good run on Minchinhampton Common. Basically a 2 in 1 pie has half pie filling and half cauliflower cheese - and is half covered with a pastry crust (there's a picture on the Dog Friendly Book website). Greg opted for the steak and mushroom 2 in 1 and I went for the pork, bacon, celery and cider with Stilton mini pie.

Wow. The pastry melts in your mouth, the cauliflower cheese is delicious and the fillings were packed with tender chunks of meat. Highly recommended. I'm so glad I had the mini pie and not the full size because we had to humbly ask for a doggy bag (happily provided) as Greg just couldn't eat the whole of his pie (and Greg can eat pies) (Don't tell him I said that - he'll never read this far if you don't tell him). You can buy the pies to take home and cook as well, so if you're self-catering and just popping in for a drink then it's definitely worth it. Everything is prepared so you don't need to worry about there not being a rolling pin. We bought one to cook at home and it worked perfectly.

The pub itself is split into smaller rooms - we were tucked away near the kitchen, which was absolutely fine, although we had to keep reminding the dog to keep her tail tucked in.

As we were paying, we noticed a jar full of dog biscuits on the bar with a note to help yourself (we didn't as she'd just wolfed down three big pieces of meat, and I don't like dog biscuits much). There's a dog bowl by the front door and the owner was more than happy to spend a few minutes telling us about the walk/cycle path starting in Nailsworth (just a few minutes by car) where we could walk all the way to Stroud if we wished.

Highly recommended!

Food served from 12pm - 9:30pm

Places to eat near walks

Geocaching Circular walk - Avening

http://www.geocachetrails.com/2011/04/trip-report-avening-circular-walk

The Bell Inn Avening

29 High Street, Avening, Gloucestershire. GL8 8NF

Telephone: 01453 836422

Website: www.thebellinnavening.co.uk

You're not too far from Hazel Woods in Avening if you want a quick walk before supper. Mains start around £10.

Food served in Pete's Bistro from 6:30pm - 9 ish.

Things to do in Dursley, Nympsfield & Uley

Dursley Farmers Market

Held every second Saturday of the month.

Walks

www.strollinginstrouddistrict.org/downloads/CCC33.pdf

Uley Bury

How to find it: Off the B4066 at Crawley Hill. There's a lay-by on the left as you go up the hill.

Iron age fort.

Hetty Peglers Tump (seriously)

How to find it: Off the B4066 (there's a brown heritage sign marked Uley Long Barrow)

Website: www.english-heritage.org.uk/daysout/properties/uley-long-barrow-hetty-peglers-tump/

Another Neolithic long barrow, named after the woman who once owned the land. Not an accidental cut and paste from my other book - a foray into Northern erotica.

Coaley Peak Viewpoint & Picnic Area & Nympsfield Long Barrow

How to find it: Off the B4066 past Uley Bury and Hetty Pegler's Tump. Follow the brown heritage signs. Plenty of car parking.

Website: www.gloucestershire.gov.uk/index.cfm?articleid=1426 or www.english-herit-age.org.uk/daysout/properties/nympsfield-long-barrow/

Another of Gloucestershire's fantastic viewpoints - on a clear day you can see the Welsh Hills. The star of the show is the Nympsfield long barrow - a Neolithic burial chamber (yep - viewpoints, forts and burial sites - we've got them all here). The pasture has been seeded with a wild flower seed mix and you'll find information boards dotted about. There's a walk through the beech woods, and the Cotswold Way also crosses through the site.

The entrance to Woodchester Park is across the road.

Woodchester Park & Mansion

Nympsfield, Stonehouse, Gloucestershire. GL10 3TS.

How to find it: Off the B4066 Stroud to Dursley Road (there is no access from the A46. The entrance to the car park is on the B4066 Stroud to Dursley Road)

Largely owned by the National Trust, Woodchester park is a beautifully secluded and offers marked walks around the lakes. Because of the dense woodland it's one of our top choices when it's particularly rainy as the trees do offer some protection. The mansion itself is a mile from the car park. This is close to where the 2012 'Wild Cat with deer munchies' sightings were, so keep your eyes peeled and you could find yourself in the Gloucestershire Echo.

Dogs must be kept under close control and on leads where requested. There is a £2 parking fee.

Coaley Point and Nympsfield Longbarrow are just across the road.

Places to eat near walks

Because this is a dog walking paradise I've listed all the places to eat as near walks... please tell us if you find more.

The Old Spot Inn

Hill Road, Dursley, Gloucestershire. GL11 4JQ

Telephone: 01453 542870

Website: www.oldspotinn.co.uk

The Old Spot was CAMRA's National real Ale Pub of the year in 2007 and also won the best cask Ale pub of 2011 at the Great British Pub awards. Their website is a touch on the busy side, but what a brilliant resource - this is the local pub we remember from years past (I did my time behind the bars in Derbyshire when growing up). There's such a sense of community - the walks page on the site is put together by the locals and I love the little comment to 'find me in the spot' from the web master if you have a problem you need to report with the website.

Anyway - we should perhaps tell you a little about the food instead of getting all dewy eyed. The pub recommend booking and there is only a small family room, so if you have children with you then it is worth phoning in advance. It is possible to eat and drink in the (covered and heated) outdoor area but given that we are in the UK I like to know my salad isn't going to be blown off my plate (I never order salad for JUST that reason). Prices start from under £10 and once again they serve home made desserts, including bread and butter pudding...

Food served 12pm - 3pm Currently no evening meals being served but this could change so it's worth calling to find out.

The Old Crown Inn

17 The Green, Uley, Dursley, Gloucestershire. GL11 5SN

Telephone: 01453 860502

Website: www.theoldcrownuley.co.uk

Good range of hot and cold meals, with hot mains starting at £9

Food served Monday - Friday 12pm - 2pm and 6pm - 9pm and all day at weekends.

The Old Fleece

Rooksmoor, Woodchester, Gloucestershire. GL5 5NB

Telephone: 01453 872582

Website: www.food-club.com/old-fleece.htm

Twitter: @Nick_and_Chris

Gastro style menu, with mains starting at the £10 mark. The team here were our rescuers, after an unsuccessful attempt to eat at a place recommended to us a bit further out. We had wanted to try the Old Fleece for a while so it was well worth doubling back on ourselves and making the effort. There was a bit of a wait for food but it was a sunny afternoon and the place was busy. I had a steak and Stilton pie with chips (I honestly didn't need the chips) - absolutely faultless. Dog bowl outside which even Skatie deigned to drink from (she's normally very fussy). Friendly team, delicious food - can't wait to go back there.

Food served 11am - 10pm every day.

The Ram Inn

Station Road, South Woodchester, Gloucestershire. GL5 5EL

Telephone: 01453 873329

Website: www.raminn-woodchester.co.uk

Another traditional village pub - roaring fires, wood floors and loads of outside seating with fabulous views. Quiz nights on Sunday starting at 8pm.

Food served 12pm - 2:30pm and 6pm - 9pm every day (except Sundays when they stop serving at 8:30pm).

The Rose and Crown Inn

3 The Cross, Nympsfield, Stonehouse, Gloucestershire. GL10 3TU

Telephone: 01453 860240

Website: www.theroseandcrowninn.com

Dogs welcome in the bar area. Straightforward menu, including a selection of lighter bites.

Food served daily from 12pm.

Things to do in Stroud

I've always felt that Stroud has a much more laid back feel than some of the other major towns in Gloucestershire. The little hamlets around the outskirts are lovely but I can't help feeling that parts of the centre are a bit like an old hippy with failing eyesight who hasn't noticed that the paint is chipping off the door frame - the centre is a tiny bit shabby in places. Don't whatever you do let this put you off - there are some great things to see in and around Stroud.

You'll find the Tourist Information Centre in the subscription rooms on George Street (Telephone: 01453 760960 or email tic@stroud.gov.uk) It's open from Monday - Saturday 10am - 5pm.

Walks

There's a huge selection of downloadable walks on the Strolling in Stroud website here: www.strollinginstrouddistrict.org/downloadablewalks.asp

Farmers Market

If you're visiting on a Saturday (and especially if you're self catering) the Stroud Farmers Market (the very first one held in Gloucestershire) runs every Saturday from 9am to 2pm in the town centre.

Stratford Park & the Museum in the Park

Stratford Road, Stroud, Gloucestershire. GL5 4AF

Approaching Stroud from Painswick (as we do) turn left at the 1st roundabout and you'll see Stratford park clearly signposted. Plenty of free car and coach parking.

Stratford Park itself is a lovely place to walk around. Well behaved dogs are very welcome outside in the park itself. It's the home of the Museum in the Park - only guide dogs are allowed inside the Museum for conservation reasons, however there is a water bowl outside and (according to the very helpful Museum Administrator we spoke to) most dogs are happy to wait outside in the courtyard for a little while.

The Cotswold Canal Visitors Centre

Bell House, Wallbridge Lock, Stroud, Gloucestershire. GL5 3JS

Telephone: 07582 286636

Website: www.cotswoldcanals.com/pages/visitor-centres/stroud.php

You'll find the canal visitor centre at the (very busy) junction of the A419 and the A46 (Follow the signs to the railway station for parking at Cheapside). We usually get hopelessly lost in Stroud, but the car parks do have street maps in situ so it's fairly easy to find your way to the canal. At the moment it's not possible to get down to the canal towpath due to the restoration project, but normally you can get down and walk. There's a cafe at the visitor centre and a dog bowl and seating outside (dogs are not allowed in the cafe). Or you might choose a seat on the roundabout. I'm actually not kidding.

Open Monday, Tuesday, Wednesday & Friday - 10am - 1pm, Thursday & Saturday - 10am - 4pm and at any time that the green flag is flying.

Places to eat

Woolpack

Slad, Stroud, Gloucestershire. GL6 7QA

Telephone: 01452 813429

Website: www.thewoolpackinn-slad.com

Mains start from £10. They actively encourage locals and fishermen with excess crop or catch to bring it to the pub.

Food served Monday 12pm - 2pm. Tuesday - Saturday 12pm - 2pm and 6:30pm - 9pm. Sunday 12pm - 3pm (booking advised).

Things to do in Wooton Under Edge

You'll find the Tourist Information Point at:

The Heritage centre

The Chipping, Wotton-under-Edge, Gloucestershire. GL12 7AD

Telephone: 01453 521541

Website: www.wottonheritage.com

Newark Park

Ozleworth, Wotton-under-Edge, Gloucestershire. GL12 7PZ

Telephone: 01793 817666

Website: www.nationaltrust.org.uk/newark-park

Another former Tudor hunting lodge with extensive gardens. Dogs welcome on a lead.

Places to eat

The Star Inn

Market Street, Wotton-Under-Edge, Gloucestershire. GL12 7AE

Telephone: 01453 844651

Website: www.the-star.co

Food served Monday - Friday 12pm - 2pm.

Swan Hotel

16 Market Street, Wotton-Under-Edge, Gloucestershire. GL12 7AE

Telephone: 01453 843004

Website: www.swanhotel.biz

Good traditional menu, with something to suit everyone, including some gluten free options.

Food served in one form or another all day.

The bit where people tell me that it's OK because 'their dog is really friendly'

In the immediate aftermath of the great flood of 2007 we did a lot of road walks - mainly because it was impossible to walk without getting covered in mud, and it was hard enough washing ourselves in a bowl of precious water, much less washing the dog.

It was soon becoming clear though that Skatie needed a bit of a run so I decided to take her up to the field. As per usual I kept her on her lead until I could see if there were any dogs already there - sure enough as we turned the corner a huge dog came belting towards her. I shouted to the owner - asking if she could call her dog back and got the usually reply 'oh don't worry - he's really friendly'.

In doggie terms, 'really friendly' seems to mean rushing up to say hello without waiting for an introduction and shoving your nose up your intended target's bottom. Try it next time you visit your local and see if people think 'blimey this person is really friendly'.

Anyway - all Skateboard saw was a dog running at her, and no means of escape, as she still had her lead on... So without warning she decided to jump into my arms, which would have been cool were it not for the fact that a) she'd never done it before, b) I wasn't expecting it and c) I had bare arms. She totally miss-timed it, raked her front claws down my throat (nice) and her back feet were scrabbling for some purchase on my right arm. I admit that I did ask a little more 'forcefully' that the dog was called off, whilst I tried to untangle Skatie's front claw from the necklace I had on, without dropping her.

I looked down and realised to my horror that she was covered in blood. I was sure the dog hadn't bitten her although the whole thing had been a whirly-gig of tooth, claw, fur, shrieks of surprise from me, and yelps from Skatie so I wasn't sure what had happened - and my chest was sore where she'd caught me with her claws. I felt at my throat and chest and could tell I wasn't cut - it was just painful. Then I felt something warm on my arm and realised where the blood had come from. We walked home as quickly as possible, with me trying not to look too closely….

When I opened the front door, Greg said 'oh that was quick', looked at the dog, looked at my arm and went 'cool - you can see all the fat poking out from under your skin - I'll go and get the car shall I?' And off we went to A&E. I ended up with 5 stitches and the kind of antibiotics that could take a horse down, due to the fact that a week previously the field had been covered in filthy flood water.

So yes - the dog was probably friendly but when I say 'please could you call your dog off' it'd be great if once in a while people did as I politely asked, instead of trying to reassure me that we've just come face to face with bloody Lassie, and they'll be romping around like old friends faster than you can say 'treat?' The reality is I'm most likely going to have to run home and get on my bike or in the car, and spend the next couple of hours trying to find my dog after she's legged it.

Also - if I'm in a pub eating my lunch and my dog backs away from your dog, next time how about you take the hint and back off as well, instead of saying 'Oh she does want to say hello really, yes she does' in a REALLY IRRITATING baby voice and releasing a bit more of your stupid extending lead. So now not only am I trying to get myself between your dog and mine whilst holding on to a plate and a glass, we've also got a tangle of lead wrapped round the treadle sewing machine that's fashionably been turned into a table. And all the time you're telling me how friendly your dog is and asking me if mine's a rescue, MY LUNCH IS GETTING COLD.

South Cotswolds

Things to do in Cirencester

To my absolute shame - and although we live 20 minutes away I had never visited Cirencester until we started researching. You'll find the Tourist Information Centre in the entrance to the Corinium Museum on Park Street (Telephone 01285 654180) where you can get a copy of a walk around Cirencester.

Cirencester Farmers Market

Takes place in the Market Place every second and fourth Saturday in the month.

Cirencester itself is a fantastic place for a bit of speciality shopping, stacks of independent shops as well as high street names. You'll find regular antique and craft fairs in The Corn Hall (26 Market Place, Cirencester, Gloucestershire. GL7 2NY) - well behaved dogs are allowed in both the arcade and the Cornhall.

Cirencester Park - Bathurst Estate

Cirencester. GL7 2BU

If you fancy a bit of greenery then the park is open to the public 8am to 5pm every day throughout the year, free of charge. Depending on events being held in the park, there may be some areas where dogs cannot be taken.

Cirencester Ampitheatre

Cotswold Avenue, Cirencester.

Website: www.english-heritage.org.uk/daysout/properties/cirencester-amphitheatre/

If you're doing 'the earthworks' tour of Gloucestershire then this is another one to tick off your list (There's an earthworks tour? really?) It's to the west of the town and is signposted. Free admission.

The Cotswold Water Park

Gateway Centre, Spine Road, South Cerney, Gloucestershire. GL7 5TL

Telephone: 01793 752413

Website: www.waterpark.org

Definitely worth picking up a guide to the water park from the tourist information centre if you get the chance. There's a bit of something for everyone, plenty of way-marked walks, bird watching, watersports, cycling... there's even a bathing beach... as well as a separate bathing beach for dogs (Follow the signs for head4heights (below)). Dogs are not allowed in the cafes, (and rather 'handily' the Gateway Information Centre is in the cafe...) but you've the option of the Bakers Arms at Somerford Keynes or the Old Boathouse at the Gateway Centre. There's also plenty of picnic areas.

Head 4 Heights Ltd

Cotswold Country Park and Beach, Spratsgate Lane, Cirencester. GL7 6DF

Telephone: 01285 770007

Website: www.head4heights.net

For the daredevils amongst you, how about testing your head for heights? Choose from a range of high rise adventures including the totem challenge and free fall... No, I've not tried ANY of them - no-one needs to see a woman in her 40s crying on the top of a pole.

Open most weekends from 10am to 5pm and every day throughout the school summer, Easter and half term holidays, from April 1st - November 1st.

Places to eat

The Crown

17 West Market Place, Cirencester. GL7 2NH

Telephone: 01285 653206

Website: www.crowniren.com

A really friendly welcome from the staff and locals alike. Skateboard ended up giving out plenty of ear kisses to a couple sat at the table next to us. The pub has lovely long scrubbed pine tables (Skateboard was particularly impressed because the previous occupants had dropped some peas, so she quickly hoovered those up) The Crown is nestled amongst the boutiques and interiors shop so it's the perfect place to eat if you've have a good walk around Cirencester and want some good home cooked food. They also do a lovely cup of tea. Sundays you can get a good roast dinner with children's portions and a vegetarian roast as well. Food is served from 12 - 9pm, and there's both wifi and BT openzone internet access available. We were disappointed not to be there for one of the impromptu sing-a-longs which apparently involves visitors and regulars...

Food served 12pm - 9pm.

The Black Horse

17 Castle Street, Cirencester. GL7 1QD

Telephone: 01285 653187

Website: www.blackhorsepubcirencester.co.uk

Slightly more 'chainy' feel to the menu here, but if you're after a quick value snack then this is a good dog (and child) friendly option. Mains from £7 with a selection of light bites around £5.

Food served all day.

Lick the Spoon

3 Black Jack Street, Cirencester. GL7 2AA

Telephone: 01285 885266

Website: www.lickthespoon.co.uk

We noticed that there is a covered seating area here, so if it's raining you do have a none pub option for a cup of tea, so long as you're not on your own as dogs are not allowed inside (obviously). In fine weather there is pavement seating outside many of the cafes on Black Jack Street.

The Fleece Hotel

Market Place, Cirencester. GL7 2NZ

Telephone: 01285 658507

Website: www.thefleececirencester.co.uk

Good bar menu, with mains around the £10 mark and a range of sharing platters. Dogs allowed in the bar area.

Food served Monday - Saturday 12pm - 9:30pm and Sunday 12pm - 8:30pm.

The Highwayman Inn

Beech Pike, Elkstone, Near Cheltenham, Gloucestershire. GL53 9PH

Telephone 01285 821221

Website: www.the-highwayman-inn.co.uk

We have driven past the Highwayman Inn hundreds of times (it's on the main A417 between Cheltenham and Cirencester). Greg regularly comes to pick me up from Swindon when I can't face the extra hour on the train home from London, and we happily sail past on our way to and from Aldbourne and Reading…

This particular Sunday I wanted to go to Caudle Green - I've read most of the books about the Mitford sisters and knew that Pamela Mitford spent the latter part of her life living there - I just wanted to see it for myself. So off we set after a bracing walk at Crickley Country park. Once we got on the A417 we were about to sail past again when Greg suggested we stop 'for a quick cup of tea'.

What a treat we've missed. As soon as we walked in it was clear that the outside does absolutely no justice to the inside of this beautiful building. Low ceilings: check. Beams: check. Roaring open fire: check. There's a cosy sofa section with low tables (which is where we initially settled as it was almost Sunday lunch time and we thought it best to avoid getting in the way), but then of course we saw the first few Sunday lunches being carried past and they looked marvellous. We quickly decided to eat, and because there are tables away from the main bar area we didn't feel like we would be disturbing other customers who may not want a pair of doe eyes staring at them as they tucked in to their roast beef. We made the decision in the nick of time as the place quickly started to fill up, with customers spilling out of the bar area to the lighter extension at the back of the Inn. The food (all home-made) was delicious - I was really impressed that the veg didn't come out as an overcooked mush - I like a bit of crunch (and Skateboard loves crunching carrots). The Highwayman Inn is also child friendly with 2 high chairs and baby changing facilities in the ladies loo.

Food served Monday - Saturday 12pm - 2pm and 6pm - 9pm. Sunday 12pm - 3pm.

The Wild Duck Inn

Drakes Island, Ewen, Cirencester, Gloucestershire. GL7 6BY

Telephone: 01285 770310

Website: www.thewildduckinn.co.uk

The Thames Path runs through Ewen www.nationaltrail.co.uk/thamespath/ so if you fancy working up a bit of an appetite you could try a stretch - although parking in Ewen is tricky at times.

Friendly staff (When I asked if they accepted dogs the bar man came back quick as a flash - "As payment? Yes!") Have a very popular steak night on Tuesdays. Mains start at £15 or try the tapas mini plates at £3 each or 4 for £10.

Food served Monday - Sunday. Light lunches 12pm - 2pm. Evening menu served 6:45pm - 10pm (except Sunday when service stops at 9:45pm).

Places to eat near walks

The Tunnel House Inn

Tarlton Road, Nr Cirencester, Gloucestershire. GL7 6PW

Telephone: 01285 770280

Website: www.tunnelhouse.com

Between the villages of Coates and Tarlton, the Tunnel House Inn is a 'Skateboard and Maggie approved' dog friendly establishment. Maggie belongs to our friends Karl and Jo and is gorgeous soft golden labrador.

Leaving Cirencester follow the signs to Tetbury and you'll see the brown heritage signs for the canal tunnel. The approach is a little bumpy - don't be put off. Child friendly as well as dog friendly with a playground, rescued ducks and two pigs in the garden. Sunday lunch is hearty with lots of vegetables and well cooked beef (and the lamb shank is also good). Leave room for the treacle tart which you can walk off on any number of the walks starting at the pub.

We chose the walk by the canal as Maggie can't go too far on rough terrain, so she kept up a gentle pace whilst Skateboard ran off ahead, then back, then off, then back until she fell in behind the pack for a gentle stroll back to the car park. If you're visiting the Cotswolds on holiday then we recommend a trip here. If you're camping with your dog then there are pitches available in the grounds of the Inn as well (see places to stay).

Mains start at around £10.

Food served all day.

The Cotswold Water Park & The Old Boathouse

Lake 6, Spine Road East, South Cerney, Gloucestershire. GL7 5FP

Telephone: 01285 864111

Website: www.oldboathousepub.co.uk

If you pull into the main entrance (signposted information centre) then you'll see the Old Boathouse on your right. There's a circular lakeside walk next to it (around lake 6) which is fairly short but plenty of wildlife to be spotted, and Skateboard enjoys a paddle in the clear water of the stream at the halfway point. Food is served all day. The Old Boathouse is billed as a gastro pub. It's certainly a really lovely friendly place - and it is trying hard but I'm not 100% convinced - yet the team were so helpful that I wanted it to be better! Seems like a good reason for me to go back and try a bit more from the menu. That said, the 'light bites' and appetizers are really good value for money if you fancy a tapas style snack.

Food served all day.

The Cotswold Water Park & The Bakers Arms

Somerford Keynes, Cirencester, Gloucestershire. GL7 6DN

Telephone: 01285 861298

Website: www.thebakersarmssomerford.co.uk

The Bakers Arms is in the Cotswold Water Park with Keynes Park beach only a short distance away. There is an entrance fee to Keynes Park Beach that varies depending on season - when we went it was £2 per car.

For the walk, follow the signs for Keynes Park Beach and enjoy one of the way-marked walks - the Bakers Arms is a little down the road (easily walkable) in Somerford Keynes.

Food is served from 12pm - 9pm every day with light meals served 12pm - 4pm Monday to Sunday.

The Trout Inn

St.John's Bridge, Faringdon Road, Lechlade on Thames, Gloucestershire. GL7 3HA

Telephone: 01367 252313

Website: www.thetroutinn.com

Dogs allowed but must stay on the flagged floor area in the bar. Check out the website - some brilliant pictures of the regulars. Lovely riverside walks nearby and a good gastro style menu, with mains starting around £14. Serves trout from Bibury Trout Farm.

Food served Monday - Saturday 12pm - 2pm and 7pm - 10pm. Sunday 12pm - 2:30pm and 7pm - 9:30pm.

Things to do in Bibury

William Morris described Bibury as the most beautiful village in England, and the row of weavers cottages called Arlington Row is possibly one of the most photographed Cotswold scenes (it'd kill me living there if I had to keep everything looking picture postcard tidy...). Bibury Church is worth a potter round as well and if you are a fan of ancient churches there's a free booklet 'Churches in and around the Fairford area' which groups the 22 churches into 'trails'.

We usually start at the trout farm then walk along the river into Bibury, then back, crossing the bridge and cutting across the front of Arlington row. This takes you down the other side of Rack Isle (now a nature reserve but previously used by the weavers to hang the cloth to dry on wooden racks - hence the name).

Bibury Trout Farm

Bibury, Cirencester, Glooucestershire. GL7 5NL

Telephone 01285 740215

Website: www.biburytroutfarm.co.uk

How to find it: Bibury is on the B4425 between Cirencester and Burford - you can't miss the trout farm as it's opposite the Swan Inn.

Open April - September 8am - 6pm, March and October 8am - 5pm November - February 8am - 4pm. Beginners fishery open weekends March - October and local school holidays - make sure you phone to confirm and book.

The Bibury Trout farm spawns up to 6 million trout ova every year. Dog friendly so long as they are kept on leads. There's a gift shop where you can buy fresh trout or you can have a go at catching your own (you will be expected to despatch your catch the traditional way and gut it yourself so be prepared). If you're visiting with children or anyone squeamish then it's best to use the main entrance as the entrance off the carpark is right next to the catch your own (they do warn you). Buy a pot of food and watch the water come to life with trout competing for the pellets - it's amazing, and reminds me of the Sundays I used to spend at the Hologram Museum in Matlock Bath when The Boy was little. The information posts are looking a bit worn, but it's a working trout farm - I could quite happily sit and watch the trout swimming round for hours.

There's a small children's playground and coffee shop selling cakes and light snacks with outside seating - half of it covered and half out in the sun. If it's full then the Swan Hotel is right across the road and as you get your hand 'stamped' you can pop out and go back in again.

Places to eat

The Swan Hotel

Bibury, Nr Cirencester, Gloucestershire. GL7 5NW

Telephone: 01285 740695

Website: www.cotswold-inns-hotels.co.uk/property/the_swan_hotel/index.htm

In summer you can eat in the courtyard, in winter there's a roaring log fire in the cosy bar that's open to non residents of the hotel. Mains hover around the £13 mark.

Food served 12pm - 2:30pm and 6:30pm - 9:30pm with an afternoon tea menu served all day.

The Kings Arms

The Street, Didmarton, near Badminton, Gloucestershire. GL9 1DT

Telephone: 01454 238245

Website: www.kingsarmsdidmarton.co.uk

Dogs are allowed in the back bar.

Food served Monday - Saturday 12pm - 2pm and 6pm - 9pm. Service stops at 8:45pm Sundays.

The Hare & Hounds Foss Cross

Chedworth, Nr Cirencester, Gloucestershire. GL54 4NN

Telephone: 01285 720288

Website: www.hareandhoundsinn.com

Twitter: @hare_hounds_inn

How to find it: Between Cirencester and Northleach

The Hare and Hounds pub is dog friendly but the accommodation is not. Mains start around the £14 mark

Food served every day from 11am - 2:30pm and 6pm - 9:30pm.

Things to do in Northleach

You're only a few minutes away from the Sherbourne Estate here and not far from Cirencester.

Although it's not massive there is stuff to see in Northleach, the church (not dog friendly) is worth a walk around, as the architecture is beautiful and the village itself is picture postcard pretty.

Places to eat

The Wheatsheaf Inn

West end, Northleach, Gloucestershire. GL54 3EZ

Telephone: 01451 860244

Website: www.cotswoldswheatsheaf.com

Twitter: @WheatsheafGL54

We turned up at half past two mid-week after a brisk walk round Northleach on a chilly January day. Roaring open fires, an eclectic hotch potch of furniture, and a superb gastro menu. Try the devilled kidneys (in fact try two plates as you won't want the first plateful to empty) Mains around the £14 mark, and if you've room and it's on the menu try the popcorn, pecan and salted caramel sundae as well (anything with nuts and popcorn is practically health food in my book).

Fantastically dog friendly team (Skateboard got a pig's ear from the huge jar behind the bar). This is in my top 10 and is well worth a visit.

Lunch : Monday to Friday 12 - 3pm. Dinner: Monday to Sunday 6pm - 10pm, (10:30pm Friday and Saturday). Brunch: Saturday and Sunday 10am - 4pm. Afternoon tea: daily 4pm - 6pm.

Note from their website: There is nothing worse than being told the kitchen is closed, wherever possible we will try to accommodate your needs, if the kitchen is still serving dessert to any table and if there is a table free then we will be very happy to feed you!

The Sherbourne Arms

Market Place, Northleach, Gloucestershire. GL54 3EE

Telephone: 01451 860241

Website: www.sherbornearms.com

Traditional pub menu, with good value mains around the £8 mark.

Food served Monday to Sunday 12pm - 2:30pm and 6:30pm - 9pm. (except Sunday 6:30pm - 8:00pm).

The Puesdown Inn

Compton Abdale, Cheltenham, Gloucestershire. GL54 4DN

Telephone: 01451 860262

Website: www.puesdown.cotswoldinns.com

As well as the bar menu, there's also a traditional pizza oven. The restaurant has appeared in the Good food guide for the last three years.

Food served 12 - 3pm and 6pm - Late every day (excluding Sundays when they stop serving at 3pm).

The Inn at Fossebridge

Fossebridge, Fosseway, Cheltenham, Gloucestershire. GL54 3JS

Telephone: 01285 720721

Website: www.cotswolds-country-pub-hotel.co.uk

Twitter: @FossebridgeInn

Food (in one form or another!) is served pretty much throughout the day starting with breakfast from 8:30am and finishing with dinner until 9pm, with lunch and cream teas in between. You should find dog biscuits on the bar as well. Gets very busy at weekends. Has a beautiful lake in the grounds that you can walk around.

The Sherborne Arms

Aldsworth, Gloucestershire GL54 3RB

Telephone: 01451 844346

Website: www.thesherbornearms.com

Yes - another Sherborne Arms. Situated on the B4425 between Burford and Bibury (not far from Northleach). Light snacks from £5.

Food served from 12pm - 2pm and 6pm - 9pm Tuesday to Saturday and 12pm - 2pm on Sundays.

Places to eat near walks

Sherbourne Estate & The Sherbourne Village shop and Tea Rooms

How to find it: On the A40 between Cheltenham and Burford, Just past Northleach. There are two signs - the brown one for the Sherbourne Estate (ignore) and the 'normal' one for Sherbourne (take this one). Coming from Cheltenham turn LEFT for Sherbourne not right for Sherbourne estate. There's often a Romany caravan and a big old shire horse on the corner, surrounded by wood carvings so you can't miss it (although I often do).

After turning off the A40, you'll find the entrance to the Sherborne estate on your right a little way up the road - the carpark is on the right. Car parking is £1 and there's an honesty box at the entrance. At the rear and to the left of the car park you'll see the information barn and a box of leaflets with a number of marked walks around the estate (if like me you're too busy watching out for small furries or interesting photographs then I find the markers really handy). We recommend (and have done) both the family fun walk and the historic farmland hike.

Make sure you keep an eye open for deer as you will come across them grazing and we don't want you doing a Fenton*. Both these walks pass the war memorial in Sherbourne itself, and just past there on the left you'll find the Sherbourne Village shop and tea rooms - absolutely well worth a stop. Tea is served in delicate china cups and the home made cakes are fantastic. You can also order quick warm snacks like baked beans and cheese on toast as well as browse the fine range of home made pastas.

Although dogs are not allowed inside, there is a water bowl outside and plenty of seating.

Three of the Sherbourne Estate walks pass the tea rooms. Worth noting (as we've been caught out), that if you are doing the family fun walk then you have to make an acute turn to walk with the church on your right at the War Memorial - otherwise you join the longer farmland hike (which Skateboard didn't mind at all but it's not really the prettiest of routes in January! Luckily we'd refuelled on tea and cake…).

If you want something a bit more substantial to eat then I'd recommend you head to Northleach where you'll find the Sherborne Arms, The Red Lion and the Wheatsheaf

* You may have seen the YouTube film from 2011 with a hapless owner chasing his dog, Fenton, through Richmond Park.

The Seven Tuns

Queen Street, Chedworth, Gloucestershire. GL54 4AE

Telephone: 01285 720242

Website: www.youngs.co.uk/pub-detail.asp?PubID=334

Apparently the 'Happiest Pub in Gloucestershire'. There are woodland walks surrounding Chedworth Roman Villa (dogs are not allowed in the Roman villa) but starting at the pub it is possible to walk towards the villa through the woods and do a circular walk.

Food served Monday - Friday 12pm - 2:30pm and 6:30pm - 9:30pm. Weekends 12pm - 3:30pm and 6:30pm - 10pm.

Things to do in Tetbury

Home to the Highgrove shop at 10 Long Street, but with plenty more in the town to see and do.

Westonbirt Arboretum

The National Arboretum, Nr Tetbury, Gloucestershire. GL8 8QS

Telephone: 01666 880220

Website: www.forestry.gov.uk/westonbirt

Twitter: @Westonbirtarb

How to find it: SW of Tetbury on the A433 (well signposted)

Ahhh Westonbirt - many a happy walk here and one particularly tense one when we took my parents and their dog Jazzy. I pestered dad over and over again to let her off the lead for a bit of an explore and uttered the immortal phrase "I mean, what can go wrong?" at which point she buggered off and refused to come back. The follow up quip about "being out of the will" was met with a strange strangled sort of choking sound, and an almost audible raise in my father's blood pressure. Whilst dad had 'A bit of a moment', mum and I set about trying to persuade Skateboard to stop running round like a loon and actually go and find Jazzy.

When Skateboard's excited, she doesn't seem to listen to commands. She registers that you're talking and that you want her to do something, so she just runs through her 'showing off' repertoire: rollover? no? paw? no? speak? no? and then she starts combining two or together (rollover with paw is quite funny as she looks as if she's doing a hammy 'shot and wounded cowboy' homage). It took us a moment to get her to sit still and listen, we got a couple more paw? no?, then off she lolloped (with me trying to act like I wasn't worried that MY dog was also completely out of sight now).

After what seemed like an age (but in reality was a couple of minutes at the most) we heard the familiar sound of crashing undergrowth and the idiot appeared, tongue lolling out and best 'I did good' face on, thankfully followed (in a much daintier fashion) by Jazzy.

We decided it might be a good idea to all go home and not mention it again.

Dogs are allowed in the Silk wood area, which covers 2/3rds of the Arboretum and has way-marked trails and walks. There are bowls outside the visitor centre but dogs are not allowed inside. Plenty of dog bins as well, so you're not carrying toxic waste for 3 miles. Admission fees vary depending on the time of year.

Places to eat

The Snooty Fox

Market Place, Tetbury, Gloucestershire. GL8 8DD

Telephone. 01666 502436

Website: www.snooty-fox.co.uk

Home to the late and much missed (judging by his facebook page) Fred the Great Dane. Really good bar menu, with mains at the £9 mark served until 9pm. Pop in and say hello to George who has joined the team from Daneline - the same Great Dane rescue charity who placed Fred in his forever home with the team at the Snooty Fox.

Food served from 12pm - 9pm.

The Hunters Hall Inn

Kingscote, Nr. Tetbury, Gloucestershire. GL8 8XZ

Telephone: 01453 860393

Website: www.oldenglishinns.co.uk/kingscote/index.php

Traditional pub grub menu, with mains around the £8 mark.

Food served all day.

Places to eat near walks

The Hare & Hounds

Westonbirt, Tetbury, Gloucestershire. GL8 8QL

Telephone: 01666 881000

Website: www.cotswold-inns-hotels.co.uk/property/hare_and_hounds_hotel/index.htm

Gastro style pub, with mains starting around the £14 mark.

Food served in Jack Hare's Bar 12pm - 2:30pm and 7pm - 9:30pm.

Good Dog

My grandparents always had dogs. From Scamp the psychopath, to Madge the Lanca-shire heeler lap dog. They're now both in their 90's and both quite frail, so I was unsure how introducing them to a jumpy idiot of a dog would go. When Skatie meets a new person there are a number of steps 1. Barking 2. Running away. 3. Barking 4. Rolling on her back for love 5. Jumping up and running away 6. More barking. Eventually she will sit next to them but (as Eddie found out) try to love her on your terms, not hers, and you'll end up with a hot cup of tea in your crotch.

Skatie always wears a harness when we're out; she's adept at slipping a collar and doesn't like to be held by the neck at all so it's the best solution. It also gives us slightly more control, so when the time came for her to meet 'the olds' she was on her lead, so I could have optimal control.

At the time they met, my grandmother wasn't able to move much, having broken her hip. I was worried that Skatie would plant her front feet in her lap and give her a huge kiss, something most people are keen to avoid.

Watching her meet my grandmother was a moment I will always treasure. We walked into the house with the command 'gently' delivered from the back of my throat so she knew I wasn't messing... and a gentler dog you could not have met. Normally going into an unfamiliar house would cause her huge anxiety, not this time. She galloped in con-fidently and her tail was wagging the moment she spied my grandmother in her chair. Very gently she walked towards her with her head down and her tail wagging, and we watched my grandmother's arthritic fingers reach out for the sweet spot at the back of Skateboard's ears. Instead of her usual mentalist behaviour, she was an oasis of calm, gently leaning against my grandmother's legs and letting her love her without a moment of hesitation.

We spent an age reminiscing about their dogs. Teddy - the cairn terrier who disrupted a cadet training exercise on Mousehold Heath by finding the teens and nipping them until they abandoned their hiding place, and Sandy who, although a quarter the size of my parents' sturdy Labrador, had insisted on carrying the same stick at the same time as her, the two of them knocking a spaniel into the canal in the process.

I hope it's clear from my witterings that I really love our dog despite her obvious short-comings, but at that moment I felt something that we don't get to feel every day. I felt proud of her for knowing just what was expected of her and just what to do, when most of the time she leaves us wondering what the heck just happened.

And saying sorry. A lot.

North Cotswolds

Covers:

Bourton-on-the-Water/The Slaughters/The Rissingtons

Burford

Chipping Campden

Guiting/Barton/Naunton

Morton-in-Marsh

Stow-on-the-Wold

The Sherborne Estate and Northleach are in the South Cotswolds section

Things to do in Bourton-on-the-Water & area

Bourton and the surrounding areas are really beautiful examples of the Cotswolds at their most picturesque - the downside is that if you ever 'forget' that it's summer and have to go and pick something up from the print finishers in Bourton, then it takes you twice as long as you anticipated because of the traffic and 'as you're here and it's nearly lunchtime you might as well stop for some fish and chips'. The only reason we avoid Bourton on summer weekends are the sheer numbers of people and that's only because of Skateboard being so mardy (this is a Derbyshire word that means... erm well mardy).

Plenty of ducks to look at and in summer it really doesn't matter if places are dog friendly or not because it's brilliant to sit outside and just watch the world go by.

There is a local website run by the Chamber of Commerce: www.bourtoninfo.com which is updated with events and an independently run Tourist Information Centre which you'll find on Victoria Street next to the perfumery. Telephone 01451 820211.

The Dragonfly Maze

Rissington Road, Bourton-on-the-Water, Gloucestershire. GL54 2EE.

Telephone: 01451 822251

Website: www.thedragonflymaze.com

Solve the clues as you travel through the maze - they form a rebus puzzle that will help you to find the hiding place of the dragonfly in the central pavilion. If you've visited Cheltenham and seen the wishing fish clock in the Regent arcade, then you'll be interested to know that the dragonfly was made by the same artist - Kit Williams (of Masquerade fame). Super dog friendly.

Summer opening times from 10am until 5:30pm. Winter opening times may vary so always best to phone and check.

Birdland Park & Gardens

Rissington Road, Boughton-on-the-water Gloucestershire. GL54 2BN

Telephone: 01451 820480

Website: www.birdland.co.uk

Open all year except Christmas Day, dogs are allowed in all areas, but must be kept on a lead at all times. Birdland houses over 500 birds including penguins (my absolute favourite) pelicans, and flamingos, as well as birds of prey, lizards and reptiles. The newly opened (In 2010) Marshmouth Nature reserve is home to frogs, toads, beetles and butterflies. This area of the park is still maturing but you will find plenty to see and do. The Penguin Cafe sells a selection of snacks/toasted sandwiches and burgers and there are covered seating areas outside, however if you're after something a bit 'slower paced' and want a proper sit down inside then you're better off heading back into Bourton to try one of the dog friendly pubs there.

Cotswold Motoring Museum & Toy Collection

The Old Mill, Bourton-on-the-Water, Gloucestershire. GL54 2BY

Telephone: 01451 821255

Website: www.cotswoldmotoringmuseum.co.uk

Home to Brum (those of you of a certain age will know who this is!) There's also collections of toys, motorbikes caravans and memorabilia. When I wrote to the museum to check they wrote back immediately to say that they love well behaved dogs and they're allowed everywhere except the office. Sounds like a perfect day out.

Open 10am - 6pm seven days a week from 10th February – 16th December.

Places to eat

The Duke of Wellington

Sherbourne Street, Bourton-on-the-water, Gloucestershire. GL54 2BY

Telephone: 01451 820539

Website: www.dukeofwellingtonbourton.co.uk

Mains start around the very reasonable £8 mark, with a very good selection of light bites as well. Separate children's menu. If you simply fancy a sit down and a cuppa (with cake) The Duke of Wellington also do a cream tea.

Food is served from 12pm - 9pm and the evening menu is available from 6pm. Traditional Sunday roast available 12 - 6pm on er...Sundays.

Things to do in Burford

Burford is in fact just over the border in Oxfordshire, but it's known as the gateway to the Cotswolds so it would be churlish to leave out such a beautiful place for the sake of a bit of geography (and with a willy nilly attitude like that it becomes clear why Miss Wilkinson threw me out of her O level class back in nineteen eightysplutter....)

Although there is plenty of free on street parking, it's hotly contested, and for the sake of a few minutes extra walk through beautiful Burford I recommend you use the main car park which is also free. Coming in from the A40, go down the hill and turn right (following the signs). There's more on street parking and a little bay of spaces next to the church, but follow the road round to find the main car park (which has human toilets as well as dog bins). Skateboard loves a minute or two pausing to look at the swans and ducks - until they spot her then it's usually time to move on. Geese can really get a pace up.

Turn either left or right out of the car park entrance, depending on if you want to start at the top or the bottom of the hill (you'll find the Tourist Information Centre by turning right and heading back to the High Street - the office is on your left).

If you're self catering, we recommend calling in at the butchers on the high street.

Call in to the Tourist Information Centre, where for a £1 you can pick up the 'Walks from Burford' brochure featuring 6 walks in and around Burford - although we were advised not to do the yellow one as someone had turned the signs around. (They're long nights round here…). You can also pick up the Burford trail leaflet for a mere 50p detailing some of the historic buildings. If it's raining, then the Tolsey Museum on the high street is worth a visit and there's covered seating for whoever has to stay outside on dog duty (to be honest it's a pleasure just sitting and watching the world go by - we often play 'spot the immaculate Hunter Wellingtons').

You're also less than 5 miles away from the Sherbourne Estate on the A40 towards Northleach and Cheltenham.

The Cotswold Wildlife Park

Burford, Oxfordshire. OX18 4JP

Telephone: 01993 823006

Website: www.cotswoldwildlifepark.co.uk

Twitter: @cotswold-wildlife-park

The Park is less than 2 miles from Burford and they do allow well behaved dogs. They must be kept on a lead and under control (which is exactly why we pre-qualified ourselves out of visiting with our dog) and they're not allowed in the bat belfry, reptile house, children's farmyard and any areas with free ranging animals.

Places to eat near walks

The circular walks from the Tourist information centre all start and finish in Burford.

The Royal Oak

26 Witney Street, Burford, Oxfordshire. OX18 4SN.

Telephone: 01993 823278

Website: www.royaloakburford.co.uk

Irish and Jacky (and their collie and wolfhound) welcome you to the Royal Oak where I'm told at times there are more dogs than customers. As you walk in the door there's a poster with pictures of retired greyhounds needing a new home, so you'll need your hardest heart. A welcoming open fire - in fact the lovely smell of the fire combined with the tempting smells from the kitchen make this pub a pleasure for the senses. Did we mention home made puddings? There are two B&B rooms available but they are very popular, so you'll need to be quick if you want to book.

Food served Friday - Monday 12pm - 9pm. Tuesday - Thursday 12pm - 2pm and 6pm - 9pm.

The Highway Inn

117 High Street, Burford, Oxfordshire. OX18 4RG.

Telephone: 01993 823661

Website: www.thehighwayinn.co.uk

Up the hill on the high street you'll find the Highway Inn. There's plenty of outdoor space but you can also take your dog in to any of the rooms in the bar/restaurant area without carpets (please give particularly muddy specimens a quick rub down). They have a daily 'pub classics' menu, as well as a more extensive menu with locally sourced produce. There's something for every appetite from light bites to a full roast on Sundays.

Food served Monday - Saturday 12pm - 2:30pm and 6pm - 9pm. (Friday and Saturday until 9:30pm). Sunday 12pm - 3pm and 6pm - 8:30pm

The Lamb Inn

Sheep Street, Burford, Oxfordshire. OX18 4LR

Telephone: 01993 823155

Website: www.cotswold-inns-hotels.co.uk/property/the_lamb_inn?/lamb

Food served 12pm - 2:30pm and 6:30pm - 9:30pm. Cold sandwiches available all day until 6:30pm

The Carpenters Arms, Fulbrook

Fulbrook Hill, Fulbrook, Burford, Oxfordshire. OX18 4BH

Telephone: 01993 823275

Website: www.carpentersarmsfulbrook.com

Twitter: @CarpentersPub

A little way out of Burford and en route of two of the walks, you'll find the Carpenters Arms at Fulbrook. The lunch menu starts from around £10 and there is a set menu of two courses for £10.95, excluding Saturdays.

Food served Wednesday - Friday 12pm - 2:30pm (12pm - 3pm Saturday and Sunday). Tuesday - Thursday 6pm - 9pm (9:30pm Friday & Saturday). Closed on Mondays.

Things to do in Chipping Campden

For an up to date list of events in Chipping Campden check out www.chippingcampden.co.uk - the official website. You'll find the Tourist Information Centre on the High Street opposite the covered market hall (built in 1627). They have a selection of guides and walks around Chipping Campden and are dog friendly (although there is some low shelving - Skateboard quite liked the look of a stuffed toy which she clearly planned on snaffling when I turned my back - when it would have quickly become 'unstuffed').

Places to eat

The Noel Arms Hotel

High Street, Chipping Campden, Gloucestershire. GL55 6AT

Telephone: 01386 840317

Website: www.noelarmshotel.com

Twitter: @noelarms

After a spot of unsuccessful geocaching we plumped for lunch at the Noel Arms and flipping heck - I'm glad we did. We'd left Skateboard's pub mat in the car, so were glad to go through to the Dover's bar where there was carpet - which she then proceeded to gronch bonio all over (thank you manager, sorry cleaner - we got as many bits up as we could). Really friendly team, lovely food (two course Sunday lunch for £16). Only gripe was totally personal - I loath orange peel so was surprised to find it in my bread and butter pudding. Skateboard didn't mind though - it meant she got loads of it once the sultanas had been taken out.

Only down point was when Skateboard decided to try and get a sing-a-long started after spotting a bit of roast beef left on my plate (it was covered in horseradish). I think the 'quiet' command is going to need some practice, although it did amuse the other customers. Lurcher owners will be familiar with the concept of sing-a-long-a-skatie.

Dogs are welcome in Dover's Bar, conservatory, coffee shop and lounge. There's also a decked outside area.

Food served Monday to Saturday: 12pm - 3pm and 6pm - 9:30pm. Sunday: 12pm - 4pm and 6pm - 9:30pm. Coffee Shop is open from 9am serving drinks and cakes.

The Red Lion Inn

High Street, Chipping Campden, Gloucestershire. GL55 6AS

Telephone: 01386 840760

Website: www.theredlioninn.org

A bit further along the main street in Chipping Campden but worth a walk along to. Traditional British pub menu, starts from around the £10 mark. Also has a seasonal menu and specials board. Lovely stone flagged floors

Food served all day.

Lygon Arms Hotel

High Street, Chipping Campden, Gloucestershire. GL55 6HB

Telephone: 01386 840318

Website: www.lygonarms.co.uk

Dogs are allowed in the bar area. Mains around the £10 mark with ever changing specials board. Lamb and beef is from their own farm.

The Ebrington Arms

Chipping Campden, Gloucestershire. GL55 6NH

Telephone 01386 593223

Website: www.theebringtonarms.co.uk

Possibly the most fun conversation I've had whilst making the initial phone calls to research the guidebook. I phoned to see if the pub was dog friendly and ended up 'talking' to a visiting dog called 'Mo' (via the landlord). Mains around the £15 mark but also a range of light bites and cream teas. Parking in Ebrington is a bit on the tight side but it's a beautiful village to walk around. Would advise that you ignore the first sign for Ebrington on the B4035 coming from Morton-in-Marsh and take the second one (with the sign for the pub by it).

Food (in some form) served all day.

Things to do in Morton-in-Marsh

Moreton-in-Marsh was built on and around the original Fosse way and was a prominent coaching route. A typical north Cotswolds village, with bustling specialist shops and a fantastic market on Tuesdays.

You'll find the Tourist Information Centre on the main High Street where you can buy leaflets with local walks for £1. The office closes at 12:30pm on a Saturday (1pm in Summer) and isn't open on a Sunday. Telephone: 01608 650881. If you don't spot it immediately it's next door to the Black Bear Pub.

Some of the pubs have a lot of firemen's memorabilia which I couldn't understand until I was told there's a large fire college down the road. So, something for the cliches, I mean ladies there....

The Rollright Stones

Website: www.rollrightstones.co.uk

How to find it: Just off the A44 (follow the signs)

Download walk 4 from the Cotswolds Area of Natural Beauty website at: www.cotswoldsaonb.org.uk/userfiles/file/Walks/WalksOnWheels_WALK4.pdf and explore the rollright stone circle. You can also download a free audio tour from the Rollright Stones website. The stones were the setting for a Dr Who episode 'The stones of blood' from back in the day when I watched Tom Baker and his doggy companion K9, and are made up of the King Stone, the King's men and the Whispering Knights. There is a small admission charge of £1 or 50p for children, which goes towards the maintenance of the site, and the path is suitable for pushchairs. You'll find toilets and a farm shop and garden centre at Wyatts (towards Great Rollright) where there is a restaurant but dogs are not allowed in there (or the shop) so if you want to eat it will have to be outside or in Moreton - however the farm shop is worth a visit.

Tuesday Market

Over 200 stalls fill the High Street.

Batsford Arboretum

Batsford Park, Morton-in-Marsh, Gloucestershire. GL56 9AB

Telephone: 01386 701441

Website: www.batsarb.co.uk

How to find it: On the A44 - follow the brown tourist signs.

Dogs must be kept on a lead throughout the entire site - which is something of a relief to Skateboard as she gets extremely stressed when loose dogs run up to her. Many a time I've put myself between her and an approaching suitor and delivered a strong 'sit!' (and they're never small dogs - always about 15 stone of slobbering gristle). I have to admit it's usually pretty effective - the last time I did it the missile pulled up sharp, and looked so surprised, that his bum was on the floor before he realised he'd done as he was told. Eat your heart out Barbara Woodhouse.

Plenty of free parking but you will have to pay to get into the arboretum itself, although you can visit the garden centre and cafe for free. Admission prices start from around £6 but depend on the time of year you visit, so check out the website.

We chose a Saturday to visit with Jill and her mum, who has to use a wheelchair to get around rougher terrain. Wheelchair users are allowed in free as there's really only one path suitable along the front of Batsford House. It's still a beautiful walk amongst the trees, and boy did we have fun with those speed bumps (sorry Mona).

Guided walks and events are listed on their website. We walked right to the far end of the arboretum and had a look round Batsford Church (More Mitford history for me) - leaving Skateboard to sit outside with Mona and enjoy the November sunshine.

There is covered outdoor seating at the Cafe (accessed through the garden centre) but despite the sunshine it was still a bit chilly, so we retreated to the nearest dog friendly establishment for lunch which you'll find in Morton-in-Marsh - a few minutes away.

Wellington Aviation Museum

British School House, Broadway Road, Moreton-in-Marsh, Gloucestershire. GL56 0BG

Telephone: 01608 650323

Website: www.wellingtonaviation.org

Anyone with an interest in Aviation History will enjoy a visit to the Wellington Aviation Museum. As it says on their website "It appears to be only one room, but for the genuine enthusiast it takes two to three hours to examine the exhibits and digest all the information concerning the nearby Royal Airforce Station, its aircraft and its past history..." Created and curated by Gerry Tyack MBE (an absolutely fascinating chap to talk to) the Wellington Aviation Museum is dog friendly 'well behaved dogs but one at a time'. The entrance fee is £2 and check out the website for a complete overview of Gerry's racing past, as well as an index of all the documents held in the museum archives. Please support this fabulous little museum if you can.

Places to eat

The Bell Inn

High Street, Morton-in-Marsh, Gloucestershire. GL56 0AF.

Telephone: 01608 651688

Website: www.thebellatmoreton.co.uk

After our fun with the wheelchair at the Arboretum, we chose the Bell Inn for our lunch. It boasts the largest outdoor space in Moreton (with dog bowl of course) and there's a selection of large outdoor games available if you wish (jenga, skittles etc). The pub dog

(Ailsa) has her own spot where she can keep an eye on things and she's obviously a big hit with the locals. There's a selection of daily newspapers by the bar, so if you're on dog duty whilst everyone else explores Moreton there's plenty to keep you occupied (there's also free wifi).

Jill and I both ate from the light bites menu (£5.95 for gammon egg and chips) and Mona had the whitebait which she said was lovely. Ailsa watched longingly as Skateboard got her treats, of course we melted and had to go over and give her some as well. The Bell Inn also offer accommodation (see places to stay).

Food is served 12pm - 2:30pm and 6pm - 9pm daily.

The Swan Inn

High Street, Moreton-in-Marsh, Gloucestershire. GL56 0LL.

Telephone: 01608 650711

Website: www.swanmoreton.co.uk

Dogs are allowed in the bar, where you can always challenge each other to a quick game of pool or darts, or you could try your hand in the skittle alley (perfect if you have a retriever). Mains around the £10 mark and a good selection of sandwiches.

Food served all day.

The Redesdale Arms

High Street, Moreton -in-Marsh, Gloucestershire. GL56 0AW

Telephone 01608 650308

Website: www.redesdalearms.com

Well behaved dogs are allowed in the Redesdale Arms bar area which has a mix of tables and comfortable seating areas. Food is served all day and they have 'themed days' so omelette Wednesday, fishy Friday etc with special offers running.

Close to the bar you'll find TVs showing the latest sport (this is by no means a 'sports bar' though - much more refined).

The Redesdale Arms is noted in some guides as offering dog friendly accommodation

- we went to check and unfortunately they've been forced to stop allowing dogs after some bad experiences. Ho Hum.

The bar menu is served from 12pm until 9pm.

White Hart Royal Hotel

High St, Morton-in-Marsh, Gloucestershire. GL56 0BA

Telephone: 01608 650731

Website: www.whitehartroyal.co.uk

Twitter: @Whitehartroyal

Dogs allowed everywhere in the White Hart except for the restaurant. Gastro style menu, with mains around £15.

Food served Monday to Saturday 11:30am - 9:30pm. Sunday 12:30pm - 9pm.

The Priory Delicatessen

Old Market Way, Moreton-in-Marsh, Gloucestershire. GL56 0AJ

Telephone: 01608 651881

Website: www.prioryrestaurantmoreton.co.uk

This was the only non-pub alternative we could find (we looked really hard - honest). Unfortunately dogs are not allowed inside, but there is covered seating outside and a bowl of water for dogs. Good place to get a warming snack if you don't want a 'pub' atmosphere when you eat. Service was a bit slow the day we were there (but the proprietor seemed to be there on her own and it was very busy). It took a little while for our food to come but it was worth the wait.

Farriers Arms

Main St Todenham, Moreton-in-Marsh, Gloucestershire. GL56 9PF

Telephone: 01608 650901

Website: www.farriersarms.com

You'll find the farriers arms next to the Church in Todenham. They do a Tuesday evening special for the very competitive price of only £6.95 and this is something different every week, but be aware that booking is absolutely essential as they usually sell out. The menu changes regularly (check the chalk board) and they also do the traditional 2 roasts on a Sunday. Local roast beef and pork with all the trimmings for £11.95 and £10.95 respectively.

Well worth a visit.

Food is served daily from 12pm - 2pm and 7pm - 9pm in the evenings (except Sundays).

Inn on the Marsh

Stow Road, Moreton-in-Marsh, Gloucestershire. GL56 0DW

Telephone: 01608 650709

Website: None

The Crown Hotel

High Street, Blockley, Nr Broadway, Gloucestershire. GL56 9EX

Telephone: 01386 700245

Website: www.crownhotelblockley.co.uk

Choose from the bar menu or restaurant menu.

Food served 12pm - 2:30pm and 6pm - 9pm.

The Greedy Goose

Salford Hill Chastleton nr Moreton-in Marsh, Gloucestershire. GL56 0SP

Telephone: 01608 646551

Website: www.thegreedygoosemoreton.co.uk

Gastro style menu, served in trendy modern surroundings. Good value set lunch menu Mondays - Thursdays and 2 for 1 on the homemade pizzas on Tuesdays and Thursdays. Bar menu starts around the £10 mark.

Food served Monday - Thursday 12pm - 3pm and 6pm - 9pm. Friday, Saturday, Sunday 12pm - 9pm.

Places to eat near walks

The Great Western Arms Hotel

Station Road, Blockley, Gloucestershire. GL56 9DT

Telephone: 01386 700362

Website: www.thegreatwesternarms.co.uk or www.hooky-pubs.co.uk/pubs/location_maps/great_western.html

Super doggie friendly pub with biscuits on the bar. Does tea and freshly ground coffee as well as Hook Norton beers. You'll find a guidebook of walks on the bar and are welcome to leave your car in the car park (order your meal in advance so it's ready for you when you return).

Super friendly new landlady Gail is doing everything she can to make the Great Western Arms the most dog and walker friendly pub in the area. If you know any great walks or walking books that you think should be added to the collection then let her know (gail@ thegreatwesternarms.co.uk). You can either eat in the restaurant or 'if it'll go in a box you can take it away'

Food served from 8am until 9:30pm. Takeaway menu served until around 11pm if there's someone available to cook (how's that for service?).

Things to do in Stow-on-the-Wold

Well we finally made it to Stow-on-the-Wold on a warmer day. Skateboard immediately made herself at home by unexpectedly dumping a two bagger on the green. Whilst conscientiously cleaning it up, I discovered that some tourists really will take a photograph of anything and it definitely wasn't my best side...

Since the withdrawal of funding for Tourist Information Centres the old one has closed down but has been replaced by the independent www.go-stow.co.uk. 12 Talbot Court, Stow-on-the-Wold, GL54 1BQ. Telephone 01451 870150. You can find it off the square - you'll see a ginnel down the side of the Talbot Inn, the new Tourist Information Centre is at the end.

The team there are really helpful. It's very dog friendly, and we were chatting about dogs for ages. There's a selection of pamphlets and booklets with walks around Stow as well as sturdier walking books and guides. You can find a downloadable map of Stow on their website here: www.go-stow.co.uk/mediapool/86/863545/data/Map_of_Stow.pdf however, as the new TIC's receive no funding to keep them going (and as they are such a valuable resource) it wouldn't harm to buy the Stow Town Trail from them (for 50p).

You can try parking in the market square but it's usually full so we tend to carry on down Sheep Street (becoming Park Street) and park in the pay & display at the bottom of the hill where it's £3.30 for two hours (parking charges apply 365 days a year).

Audio Walking tour of Stow

You can purchase them from www.walkingpast.co.uk/main.html

Shopping

Home of Scotts of Stow. There's plenty of niche shopping to be had - loads of antique shops and some 'must visits' like Miette artisan chocolate (www.miette.co.uk) on Digbeth Street. You can't take dogs in unfortunately, as they produce the chocolates on site, but try their salted liquorice - it's amazing.

Have a cream tea

We've discovered 3 tea rooms in Stow that welcome dogs and they are:

Cotswold Garden Tea Rooms

Digbeth Street. Stow-on-the-Wold, Gloucestershire GL54 1BN

Telephone: 01451 870994

Website: www.cotswoldgardentearooms.co.uk

Lovely selection of home made cakes and outdoor seating if you're there in the summer.

New England Coffee House

1 Digbeth Street, Stow-on-the-Wold, Gloucestershire. GL54 1BN

Telephone: 01451 831171

Website: www.newenglandcoffeehouse.co.uk

As well as tea and coffees you'll find milkshakes, hot chocolates and free wi-fi. This is slap bang opposite Miette chocolate shop...

Ann Willow Tea Shop

11 Market Square, Stow-On-The-Wold, Gloucestershire. GL54 1BQ

Telephone: 01451 830000

If you're visiting Stow in high season then you'll have to be quick to get the bay window looking out over the square. Good value food (ham, egg and saute potatoes £5.50).

Places to eat

The Eagle and Child

The Royalist Hotel, Digbeth Street, Stow-on-the-Wold, Gloucestershire. GL54 1BN

Telephone: 01451 830670

Website: www.theroyalisthotel.com

This gastro pub is attached to the Royalist Hotel in Stow - which is thought to be the oldest hotel in the UK.

Lovely stone flagged floors and nooks and crannies to tuck yourself away in at the Eagle and Child. Again, it's a gastro style menu, with mains around the £12 mark. Definitely one we'll be going back to for food.

Food served 6pm - 9pm.

The Talbot

The Square, Stow-on-the-Wold, Gloucestershire. GL54 1BQ

Telephone: 01451 870934

Website: www.thetalbot.net (you really need to check out this website - it's fair to say that the landlord's character really shines through).

When we visited we were both chortling at the signs and posters from the landlord dotted about the place e.g. "Thanks for reading this far, I never do" Another good modern interior (Reminded me a bit of the Falcon in Painswick) and a good sized bench table that seats 12. Gastro style menu, with mains hovering around the £13 mark.

Food served 12pm - 2:30pm and 6:30pm - 9:30pm.

The Queens Head

The Square, Stow-on-the-Wold, Gloucestershire. GL54 1AB

Telephone: 01451 830563

Website: www.donnington-brewery.com

Lovely pub serving excellent food and ales from the Donnington brewery who own a number of pubs throughout the Cotswolds. Dogs welcome throughout the bar area.

Food served 12pm - 2:30pm and 6:30pm - 9pm.

The Kings Arms

Market Square, Stow-on-the-Wold, Gloucestershire. GL54 1AF

Telephone: 01451 830364

Website: www.kingsarmsstow.co.uk

Twitter: @kingsarmsstow

You absolutely can't miss the Kings Arms. We decided that this was going to be our eatery of choice this particular week, due to me having a hankering for roast beef with all the trimmings. I'd cunningly left Skateboard's 'pub mat' in the car, which meant she wasn't going to lie down until there was something soft for her to settle on - she eventually slept on my fleece (I've created a monster).

Lovely rare roast beef with crispy roast potatoes and an assortment of veg served in a copper pot - I think this is probably the best Sunday roast veg selection I've had so far. Extra gravy came separately. We'd left the regulation treats at the side of our plates and when we were finished Skatie got hers... and a bonus as the landlady came out of the kitchen with some extra scraps of beef for her. Highly recommended. Sunday roast at around the £13 mark with a good selection of specials and light bites as well.

Food served Sunday - Monday 12pm - 9:30pm. Friday and Saturday 12pm - 10pm.

The Old Stocks Hotel

The Square, Stow-on-the-Wold, Gloucestershire. GL54 1AF

Telephone: 01451 830666

Website: www.oldstockshotel.co.uk

Good range of either snacks or main meals served in the bar (dogs are not allowed in the restaurant). Snacks start at under £5 and the main meals are good value for money starting well under £10.

The Grapevine

Sheep Street, Stow-on-the-Wold, Gloucestershire. GL54 1AU

Telephone: 01451 830 344

Website: www.thegrapevinehotel.com

Dogs welcome in the Gigot Bar - lovely gastro menu, with mains around the £13 mark.

Food served 6pm - 9pm.

Places to eat near walks

The Golden Ball Inn

Lower Swell, Gloucestershire. GL54 1LF

Telephone: 01451 833886

Website: www.thegoldenballinn.com

The Golden Ball Inn has two circular walks to download from their website.

The Golden Ball is also on the route of the shorter circular walk from Stow-on-the-Wold that you can download the audio guide from on www.walkingpast.co.uk.

Oh - and they have an Aunt Sally! Mains from around £9.

Food served 6:30pm - 8:30pm.

The Fox Inn, The Green, Broadwell

The Green, Broadwell, Nr Stow-on-the-Wold, Gloucestershire. GL56 0UF

Telephone: 01451 870909

Website: www.pubs2000.com/fox_walkers_menu.htm

Slap bang on the Village green with a brook at the end of the garden. Close to the Donnington Way. Dogs must be kept on a lead due to the pub cat (which is probably harder than Skateboard).

Food served Monday - Saturday 11:30am - 2pm and 6:30pm - 9pm. Sunday 12pm - 2pm.

Maugersbury Manor - short loop

If you've parked in the pay & display car park on the A426 you'll notice that a path runs parallel with the right hand side - this tree lined footpath will take you to the little village of Maugersbury and you can do a circle back up to Stow then choose a pub to eat in.

Warning

It's rare that Skateboard gets told off. She is the typical indulged mutt, and gets away with absolute murder.

She's never left for more than 5 hours (although we often leave her and return to find her in exactly the same position - right down to the tongue lolling over the edge of the basket) but every now and again, we have to be 'a bit stern'. And that's when we get the canine equivalent of a horse's head on your pillow.

Usually it's shoes. She'll find a favourite pair of shoes and take just one of them, but she doesn't hide it, instead she puts it somewhere we know we'll find it, like the top of the stairs or in the middle of the bed. There won't be a mark on it.

It's just to remind us what she could have done.

Introduction to Places to Stay

What we've done here is tried to find the best independent accommodation, where you can book direct without going through a booking agent (and getting half a dozen brochures from them for the rest of your life).

We did ask one smaller holiday cottage management company to give us a call as their properties looked smashing, however it was difficult to work out which ones were dog friendly and which ones weren't and we didn't want to confuse people. Anyway - they didn't call back so they're not in :)

We also phoned and spoke to most of the owners. Those who didn't seem hugely excited about the prospect of having dogs to stay (despite being listed as dog friendly) were quietly removed from the list - purely because there's nothing more stressful for both the owner of the accommodation, the owner of the dog and the dog, if everyone's on edge about muddy footprints or sicking up a rabbit (although Skateboard is more likely to sick up chewed underpants).

We've organised this section by main area and then type of accommodation, as we thought anyone looking for a hotel isn't going to want to know about camp sites, and when it's so easy to get from one end of the Cotswolds to another, it seemed that there was little point in splitting it up by town. I'm sure our reviews will tell us whether we've got this assumption right or not...

We've put some ballpark prices in where they've been available - this tends to be based on the price around May time - if you're looking for somewhere to stay in the 6 week holidays don't come back and shout at me when we're nowhere near... We only put them in as a guide - of course they change all the time, but I hate phoning up for a hotel room on the basis of a nice website, then needing a lie down when I've found out how much it's going to cost me. If however, it's only possible to find out the price by going through some convoluted booking system, then we've walked the dog instead. Life is too short for complicated web forms.

As you can imagine there are very few reviews in this section because we actually live here - if you've stayed at one of the places listed and fancy seeing your name in print, then feel free to drop us a line.

If you own dog friendly accommodation and we've not listed you then please get in touch and let us know at editor@dogfriendlybook.co.uk.

Forest of Dean - Places to Stay

Hotels & Inns

The Speech House Hotel

Coleford, Gloucestershire. GL16 7EL
Telephone: 01594 822607
Website: www.thespeechhouse.co.uk
Twitter: @speechhouse

Former Charles II Hunting Lodge. Dogs welcome in gardens and Orangery, plus Courtyard accommodation subject to availability. Prices vary and they do a number of short break special offers, so it's best to check their website.

Forest House

Cinder Hill, Coleford, Gloucestershire. GL16 8HQ
Telephone: 01594 832424
Website: www.forest-house.co.uk
Twitter: @forestbluebell

B&B but with Bluebell restaurant attached. Prices from £75 per room per night.

Tudor Farm Hotel

High Street, Clearwell, Gloucestershire. GL16 8JS
Telephone: 01594 833046
Website: www.tudorfarmhousehotel.co.uk
Twitter: @tudorfarmhouse

Dogs are allowed in the Byre Suite (and owners will be asked to sign a contract). All dogs must be kept on a lead whilst around the grounds as there are livestock in the fields. Doggy bins are also provided. Up to 2 dogs or 3 small dogs. Prices from £100 B&B.

Wyndham Arms Hotel

Clearwell, Near Coleford, Gloucestershire, GL16 8JT
Telephone: 01594 833666
Website: www.thewyndhamhotel.co.uk

Dogs welcome throughout except for the restaurant. You can leave dogs unattended in your room whilst you go for breakfast (at your own discretion). Prices from £75 B&B.

The Fountain Inn
Fountain Way, Parkend, Nr. Lydney, Gloucestershire. GL15 4JD
Telephone: 01594 562189
Website: www.fountaininnandlodge. co.uk

Bed & breakfast accommodation from £62 per night for a double room.

The Rising Sun,
Moseley Green, Parkend, Lydney, Gloucestershire. GL15 4HN
Telephone: 01594 562008
Website: www.therisingsuninn-moseley-green.co.uk
Contact: Avis & Michael Robinson

Wheelchair accessible twin room with wet room. From £50 per night.

Bed & Breakfast

Ferndale House
Upper Lydbrook, Gloucestershire. GL17 9LQ
Telephone: 01594 861294
Website: www.ferndale-house.co.uk

Double room from £58.

Symonds Yat Rock Lodge
Hillersand, Coleford, Gloucestershire. GL16 7NY
Telephone 01594 836191
Website: www.rocklodge.co.uk

Both B&B and self catering apartments. B&B from £65 per room (discount for single occupancy). Self catering from £420 per week but make sure you check the website for special offers.
No additional charge for dogs.

Millingbrook Lodge

High Street, Aylburton, Lydney,
Gloucestershire. GL15 6DE
Telephone: 01594 842163
Website: www.millingbrooklodge.com

£52.50 - £75 based on 2 people sharing.
Dogs allowed in some rooms at an additional cost of £4 per night. Check in at the
George Inn next door.

Grove Farm

Bullo Pill, Newnham, Gloucestershire.
GL14 1EA
Telephone: 01594 516304
Website: www.grovefarm-uk.com
Contact David & Penny Hill

From £35 per person per night.

Self Catering

The General Stores

Mill End, Mitcheldean, Gloucestershire.
GL17 0HP
Website: www.millendmitcheldean.co.uk

Dogs are allowed, though not upstairs.
This one's a belter if you're planning a
family get together. You can either book
the whole of the General Stores for a 2
day weekend for £2,000 - it sleeps up to
25 people. Did we mention there's a hot
tub? We didn't? There's a hot tub! Alternatively you can book George Cottage
(which sleeps up to 8) for £350 for a 3
night weekend.

Woodland Barn

Littledean Hill Road, Cinderford,
Gloucestershire. GL14 2BW
Telephone: 01594 822272
Website: www.woodlandbarn.com
Twitter: @woodlandbarn101

Sleeps up to 4 people, up to two dogs allowed at no extra charge. From £455 per
week.

The Miners Arms Cottage

The Bay, Whitecroft, Forest Of Dean, Gloucestershire. GL15 4PE
Telephone: 01594 562 483
Website: www.minersarmswhitecroft.com/holiday-cottage/

Sleeps 2 - 4. Well behaved dogs welcome. From £370 pw - right next door to the pub.

The Mount Annexe

Hillersand, Coleford, Gloucestershire. GL16 7NY
Telephone: 01594 839141
Website: www.mountannexe.co.uk

Accommodation from £250-420 per week. Dogs are £10 per week.

Symonds Yat Rock Lodge

Hillersand, Coleford, Gloucestershire GL16 7NY
Telephone 01594 836191
Website: www.rocklodge.co.uk

Both B&B and self catering apartments. B&B from £65 per room (discount for single occupancy).
Self catering from £420 per week but make sure you check the website for special offers.
No additional charge for dogs.

Oatfield Country Cottages

Oatfield Farm, Etloe, Blakeney, Gloucestershire. GL15 4AY
Telephone: 01594 510372
Website: www.oatfieldfarm.co.uk

Five self catering cottages all sleep between 2 & 4 people. Prices from £325 - £1195 depending on cottage & season.

Highbury Coach House

Bream road, Lydney, Gloucestershire. GL15 5JH
Telephone: 01594 842339
Website: www.highburycoachhouse.co.uk
Contact: Anthony & Inez Midgely

Three spacious apartments in the listed coach house of Highbury House. Close to Dean Forest and Wye Valley. Large dog friendly garden and games room with snooker table.
Stable apartment sleeps 4, Carriage apartment sleeps 3-5, Garden apartment sleeps 2.
From £200 a week. Pets by prior arrangement.

Whitemead Forest Park

Parkend, Lydney, Gloucestershire.
GL15 4LA
Telephone: 0845 3453425
Website: www.csmaclubretreats.co.uk

Open all year. Available for camping & caravanning, or stay in one of their log cabins or apartments on site. Prices vary greatly throughout the season and depending on the accommodation you require so best to check the website.

Noxon Pond Cottage

Noxon Farm, Bream Avenue, Lydney,
Gloucestershire. GL15 6QR
Telephone: 01594 562236
Website: www.noxonpondcottage.co.uk
Contact: David or Caroline

Sleeps up to 4 people, next to a carp fishing pond. 1 well behaved dog by arrangement at an additional cost of £20 per week. From £265 per week.

Camping/Caravanning/Tourers

Greenway Farm Camping & Caravan Site

Puddlebrook Road, Drybrook,
Gloucestershire. GL17 9HW
Telephone: 01594 544877
Website: www.greenwayfarm.moonfruit.com

Open April to January. Great selection of walks available to download from their website.

Pelerine

Ford House Road, Newent,
Gloucestershire. GL18 1LQ
Tel: 01531 822761
Website: www.newent.biz
Contact: Gail

Open 1st March to November.

Bracelands Caravan & Camping Park Forest Holidays

Bracelands Drive, Christchurch, Coleford, Gloucestershire. GL16 7NN
Telephone: 01594 837258
Website: www.campingintheforest.co.uk/our_sites_locations/england/forest_of_dean/bracelands.aspx

Open 1st April to 31st October.

Easy access to signposted forest trails and good access to cycle trails.

Christchurch Caravan And Camp Site Forest Holidays

Bracelands Drive, Christchurch, Coleford, Gloucestershire. GL16 7NN
Telephone: 01594 837165
Website: www.campingintheforest.co.uk/our_sites_locations/england/forest_of_dean/christchurch.aspx

Open all year.
Another camping in the forest site.

Cherry Orchard Farm Camp Site

Newland, Coleford, Gloucestershire. GL16 8NP
Telephone: 01594 832212
Website: www.cherryorchardfarm.co.uk

Caravans are welcome, but no mains hookup.

Beanhill Farm

Clanna Cross Roads, Alvington, Lydney, Gloucestershire. GL15 6AE.
Telephone: 01594 529113
Website: www.beanhillfarm.co.uk

Also a trout fishery. Solar panels make the campsite self sufficient in electricity. Dogs allowed in tents and caravans but not in the log pods. Open March - middle of October.

Plusterwine Farm

Station Road, Woolaston, Lydney, Gloucestershire. GL15 6PN
Telephone: 01594 529338
Website. www.plusterwinefarm.co.uk

Open all year. It's a working farm so dogs must be kept under control. Surrounded by beautiful walks.

Whitemead Forest Park

Parkend, Lydney, Gloucestershire.
GL15 4LA
Telephone: 0845 3453425
Website: www.csmaclubretreats.co.uk/
holidayparks/whitemead/index.php

Open all year.

Available for camping & caravanning.

Winchcombe, Tewkesbury & Broadway - Places to Stay

Covers: Tewkesbury, Winchcombe, Snowshill, Broadway

Hotels & Inns

The Bell Hotel

Church Street, Tewkesbury,
Gloucestershire. GL20 5SA
Telephone: 01684 293293
Website: www.oldenglishinns.co.uk/
tewkesbury/

Dogs welcomed at no extra charge. 24 rooms available. Prices from £65

Brook Hotel

Lincoln Green Lane, Tewkesbury,
Gloucestershire. GL20 7DN
Telephone: 01684 295405
Website: www.brook-hotels.co.uk/hotels/
tewkesbury-park-hotel-golf-and-country-club

The Brook Hotel has a specific room with patio doors which is allocated for dogs. There are some restrictions. Dogs are not allowed in any public areas within the hotel, rooms only and they are not allowed on the golf course but there are designated walking areas. If you want to eat, then you'll have to eat elsewhere or order room service. Book well in advance to take advantage of their advanced room rate.

The Lower Lode Inn

Forthampton, Gloucestershire.
GL19 4RE
Telephone: 01684 293224
Website: www.lowerlodeinn.co.uk

Within walking distance of Tewkesbury there are 4 en-suite guest rooms sleeping 1 - 4 per room. Prices from £55 for a double. Dogs must be kept under control at all times.

The Broadway Hotel

The Green, Broadway, Worcestershire.
WR12 7AA
Telephone: 01386 852401
Website: www.cotswold-inns-hotels.
co.uk/broadway

Prices from £99 but do check their website for advanced booking rates.

Horse & Hound Inn

54 High Street, Broadway,
Worcestershire. WR12 7DT
Telephone: 01386 852287
Website: www.horse-and-hound.co.uk

Has 5 en-suite guest rooms - Supplement of £10 per dog per night. Prices from £70 per room based on 2 people sharing.

The Lygon Arms Hotel

Broadway, Worcestershire. WR12 7DU
Telephone: 01386 852 255
Website: www.barcelo-hotels.co.uk/hotels/central-england/barcelo-the-lygon-arms-hotel-cotswolds

Part of the Barcelo chain (yeah you probably guessed that from the website URL) but we've found that the Barcelo group are pretty relaxed about dogs in most of their hotels. Please let them know at the time of booking that you're taking your dog. Perfect place if you fancy a bit of a treat as there is a spa at the hotel... 4 Star hotel - 4 star rates although they do have some deals on their website with rooms starting from £120.

Dormy House Hotel

Willersley Hill, near Broadway,
Worcestershire. WR11 7TS
Telephone: 01386 881240
Website: www.dormyhouse.co.uk
Twitter: @DormyHouse

Rooms from £190 per night.

The Crown Hotel Blockley   (See North Cotswolds)

The White Hart Inn
High Street, Winchcombe,
Gloucestershire. GL54 5LJ
Telephone 01242 602359
Website: www.whitehartwinchcombe.
co.uk

Sister pub to The Beehive in Montpellier and part of the Hatton Hotels group (which includes the Snooty Fox in Tetbury and the Hatton Court on the outskirts of Gloucester). As well as standard & luxury double rooms they also have 'Rambler rooms' with shared facilities (from £39). Standard Double rooms start from £49.

The Plough Inn at Ford
Temple Guiting, Cheltenham,
Gloucestershire. GL54 5RU
Telephone: 01386 584215
Website: www.theploughinnatford.co.uk

The B&B rooms overlook the gallops of Jonjo O'Neil's training yard and well behaved dogs are welcome. We also recommend the Plough Inn as one of our places to eat. From £80 per night for a double.

Bed & Breakfast

Tally Ho Bed & Breakfast
20 Beckford Road, Alderton,
Gloucestershire. GL20 8NL
Telephone: 01242 621482
Website: www.cotswolds-bedandbreakfast.co.uk

From £65 - £70 with breakfast.

Deerhurst Bed & Breakfast
Deerhurst Priory, Deerhurst,
Gloucestershire. GL19 4BX
Telephone 01684 293358
Website: www.deerhurstbandb.co.uk

A working farm, Deerhurst priory adjoins the ancient Saxon Priory Church of St Mary. It's an open plan design with twin beds so you won't be fighting over the duvet after taking in all that fresh air. From £30 per person per night.

Willow Cottage

Shuthonger, Tewkesbury,
Gloucestershire. GL20 6ED
Telephone: 01684 298599
Website: www.tewkesburybedandbreak-fast.co.uk

Prices from £50 per night.

Cowley House

Church Street, Broadway,
Worcestershire. WR12 7AE
Telephone: 01386 858148
Website: www.cowleyhouse-broadway.co.uk
Contact: Joan Reading

Rooms from £75. Well behaved dogs are welcome in the Chawton Room and are subject to an additional charge of £5 per dog per night.

The Olive Branch Guest House

78 High Street, Broadway,
Worcestershire. WR12 7AJ
Telephone: 01386 853440
Website: www.theolivebranch-broadway.com
Contact: David and Pam Talboys

From £82 per room per night.

Whiteacres

Station Road, Broadway, Worcestershire.
WR12 7DE
Telephone: 01386 852320
Website: www.broadwaybandb.com
Contact: Jenny & Stan Buchan

Useful link on their website with information about what's on in Broadway and the surrounding area. Winner of the AA good breakfast award (and if you check the website you can see why!).
Single occupancy starts at £55 and double occupancy £75.

North Farmcote B & B

Winchcombe, Cheltenham,
Gloucestershire. GL54 5AU
Telephone: 01242 602304
Website: www.northfarmcote.co.uk

Situated on the outskirts of Winchcombe in the small hamlet of North Farmcote is the home of Farmcote herbs as well as a dog friendly Country House B&B. They don't offer evening meals, but the Plough Inn at Ford do (just 2.5 miles away) and they are also dog friendly. The Cotswold way runs through the farm running down to Hailes Abbey (see things to do). From £70 per night.

Self Catering

Vine Tree Self Catering Cottage

Gander Lane, Teddington,
Gloucestershire. GL20 8JA
Telephone: 07786 438386
Website: www.countrycottagescotswolds.co.uk
Contact: Chris

Pets are allowed in the self catering cottage but not in the B&B. Please notify in advance if you are bringing pets. Two double bedrooms & one twin room, although there is also a sofa bed and futons can be placed on the minstral's gallery allowing up to 10 to be accommodated. Prices from £350 per week.

The Dovecote

Courtyard Cottages
Upper Court, Kemerton,
Gloucestershire. GL20 7HY
Telephone: None given
Website: www.uppercourt.co.uk

Sleeps 2. Dogs are allowed in the Dovecote & must be kept on a lead in the grounds.
Doggy charge of £3 per night. Prices from £600.

Lemon Tree Cottage Broadway

Full address will be given at time of booking.
Telephone: 07828 150375
Website: www.lemontreecottage.net

A mile from the Centre of Broadway the cottage is link detached to the owners property.

Dogs £10 per dog per week. Maximum of 2 by prior arrangement - have a look at their website for photos of previous doggie guests. Sleeps 4 adults. From £380 pw.

Laburnam Cottage

Church Street, Broadway,
Worcestershire, WR12 7AE
Telephone: 01386 853202
Website: www.cotswoldholidays.co.uk

Sleeps 4. Dogs by arrangement. Owned by the Crown & Trumpet which is a dog friendly pub. Prices from £645 per week. Meals available at the pub.

Burhill Cottages (3 cottages)

Burhill, Buckland, Nr Broadway,
Worcestershire. WR12 7LY
Telephone: 01386 853426
Website: www.burhill.co.uk

Three cottages set in their own grounds with a swimming pool that can be booked (for you - not your dog - although if your dog is anything like Skateboard trying to get them anywhere near a swimming pool would mean paying to have the floor relaid). Prices from £368 pw.

Russell Cottage Broadway

Telephone: 01386 858147
Website: www.cotswoldholiday.com/more_info.php?pid=61

Central Broadway. Sleeps 4 one double - one twin. Two small/one medium sized dog welcome.
From £480 per week.

Muir Cottage & The Bothy

Postlip Stables, Winchcombe,
Gloucestershire. GL54 5AQ
Telephone: 01242 603124
Website: www.thecotswoldretreat.co.uk

The Cotswold way is only metres away from the cottages at Postlip.
From £300 pw. Pets by arrangement.

One The Coates

1 The Coates, Winchcombe,
Gloucestershire. GL54 5NJ
Telephone: 07747 696098
Website: www.onethecoates.com

Three bedroom self catering holiday
home, sleeps 6. Prices from £625.

Rosemary's Cottage

Winchcombe, Gloucestershire.
Telephone: 01993 830484
Website: www.rosemaryscottages.co.uk/
thecottage-r.html

Two bedroom cottage. High season from
£395 to £475. Pets welcome at a small additional charge.

Camping/Caravanning/Tourers

The Lower Lode Inn

Forthampton, Gloucestershire.
GL19 4RE
Telephone: 01684 293224
Website: www.lowerlodeinn.co.uk

As well as dog friendly accommodation
in the pub there are pitches available for
both camping and caravans at the Lower
Lode Inn.

The Willows

Lower Lode, Forthampton,
Gloucestershire. GL19 4RE
Telephone: 01905 771018
Website: www.thewillowscaravanpark.
co.uk

Touring season 1st April to January 5th.
22 pitches. Also 14 tent pitches.

Croft Farm Waterpark

Bredons Hardwick, Gloucestershire.
GL20 7EE
Telephone: 01684 772321
Website: www.croftfarmleisure.co.uk

Open March - Mid November. Dogs must be kept on a lead and under control. However, there is a dog compound where you can exercise your dog without the worry of it running off (or falling in the lake!). Free fishing available to all campers (make sure you have a valid licence) and don't forget the watersports centre.

Leedons Caravan Holiday Home and Hire Park Broadway

Childswickham Road, Broadway,
Worcestershire. WR12 7HB
Telephone: 01386 852423
Website: www.allenscaravans.com

Open 1st March to 31st December.

Winchcombe Camping And Caravanning Club Site

Brooklands Farm, Alderton,
Gloucestershire. GL20 8NX
Telephone: 01242 620259

Open March to January - please call for specific dates.

Cheltenham - Places to Stay

Hotels & Inns

The Montpellier Chapter

Bayshill Road, Montpellier, Cheltenham. GL50 3AS
Telephone 01242 527788
Website: www.themontpellierchapterhotel.com

Fabulous boutique hotel. Rooms from £130 but check the website for packages and short breaks.

Charlton Kings Hotel

London Road, Cheltenham. GL52 6UU
Telephone: 01242 231061
Website: www.charltonkingshotel.co.uk

This smashing hotel is only a few minutes from the Dowdeswell reservoir with excellent dog walking - you can either try the 25 mile circular walk around Cheltenham or you might just prefer a run through the woods! There's a public footpath up the side of the hotel which leads to an open field for exercise. Friendly owners with resident dog. Prices from £90.

Cotswold Grange Hotel

Pittville Circus Road, Cheltenham. GL52 2QH
Telephone: 01242 515119
Website: www.cotswoldgrange.co.uk

Close to Pitville Park for doggy exercise, the Cotswold Grange Hotel is a great base for enjoying Cheltenham on foot. Just a few minutes walk and you're in the centre of town. Prices from £75.

The Big Sleep Hotel

Wellington Street, Cheltenham GL50 1XZ
Telephone: 01242 696999
Website: www.thebigsleephotel.com

A special mention for the Big Sleep Hotel. In May 2012 there was a huge gas explosion on the street we live in. We ended up being evacuated, and were taken late at night to the Big Sleep hotel, where we were looked after fantastically.

Holiday Inn Express

Dunalley Street, Cheltenham. GL50 4AP
Telephone: 01242 548200
Website: www.hiexcheltenham.com

No frills but comfortable chain hotel. For evening toileting (for fido - it's not THAT no frills) your nearest green space is the garden in the middle of Clarence Square (walk down Dunalley Street away from the Brewery Complex and turn right at the end). The advantage of being in the centre of town may be outweighed by the noise that inevitably accompanies that.

Rising Sun Hotel

Cleeve Hill, Cheltenham. GL52 3PX
Telephone: 01242 676281
Website: www.oldenglishinns.co.uk/
cheltenham/

Has two rooms dedicated to travellers staying with pets. Prices from £75

The Greenway Hotel & Spa

Greenway Lane, Cheltenham. GL51
4UG
Telephone: 01242 862352
Website: www.thegreenwayhotelandspa.
com
Twitter: @greenwayhotel

Dogs allowed in specific rooms in the coach house but not in public areas of the hotel since the hotel came under new management. Meh.

B&B

Hope Orchard

Gloucester Road Staverton, Cheltenham.
GL52 6TS
Telephone: 01242 269968
Website: www.hopeorchard.co.uk

Although a little outside Cheltenham, Hope Orchard is thoroughly approved by Jazz. Excellent Breakfasts and friendly hosts Graham & Elizabeth.

Our Review:

"The Orchards is run by enthusiastic dog lovers. Guests and their dogs stay in purpose built individual chalets. These are single rooms with en suites. They are quite basic but comfortable, and dogs may be left in them on their own. There is a large grassed area for dogs and their owners, which is adjacent to the chalets and away from the road."

Badger Towers

133 Hales Road, Cheltenham. GL52 6ST
Telephone: 01242 522583
Website: www.badgertowers.co.uk

Another Jazz approved B&B, this time a gentle walk away from the centre of Cheltenham. You'll find the Queen Elizabeth playing fields close by if your dog needs to burn off any extra energy, although Skateboard much prefers Sandford park. It is a little further away (follow the signs for Sandford Lido from Oxford Road) but it's worth the extra effort as the footpath follows the River Chelt into the town centre. From £75 for a double room.

Our Review:

"This a friendly hotel, with good quality food, and clean and pleasant rooms.

If you stay at Badger Towers you will all be made welcome, and your well-behaved dog may stay in your room whilst you eat your breakfast. We thoroughly recommend Badger Towers".

White Lodge B&B

Hatherley Lane, Cheltenham. GL51 6SJ.
Telephone: 01242 242347
Website: www.whitelodgebandb.co.uk

Two doubles & two twins - all en-suite. Prices from £65.00. One time extra charge of £5 per dog per stay.

Garden House

24a Christ Church Road, Cheltenham.
GL50 2PL
Telephone: 01242 522525 or 07979
036262
Website: www.gardenhousebb.co.uk
Contact: Miggi Lorraine

Stylishly renovated coach house in central Cheltenham in a quiet tree lined road close to Montpellier and the railway station. Guests arriving by train are collected from the station. English and Continental breakfasts are served. Price from £80 per night.

Self Catering

Balcarras Farm Cottages

Charlton Kings, Cheltenham. GL52 6UT
Telephone: 01242 584837
Website: www.balcarras-farm.co.uk
Contact: Judith & David Ballinger

There are 3 separate cottages having shared use of 3 acre grounds.
Sleeps 1 - 4. P. ts by arrangement £280 - £430 per week. Some good walks nearby at Dowdeswell Reservoir.

Church Court Cottages

Mill Street, Prestbury, Cheltenham.
GL52 3BG
Telephone: 01242 573277
Website: www.churchcourtcottages.
co.uk

Situated in the outskirts of Cheltenham in Prestbury (on the way to Winchcombe). Prestbury is reported to be one of the UK's most haunted villages. Dogs are welcome in Cleeve cottage at an additional charge of £25 per week. Prices from £900 per week.

The Coach House

9 Montpellier Parade, Cheltenham.
GL50 1UA
Telephone: 01242 248177
Website: www.cheltenhamshortbreaks.
co.uk/the-coach-house/

Situated in the centre of Montpellier so you are in the heart of the town. Sleeps 2. Price from £130 pn.

The Garden Flat
14 Eldorado Road, Cheltenham.
GL50 2PT.
Telephone: 01242 248177
Website: www.cheltenhamshortbreaks.
co.uk/the-garden-flat/

A little further out of Cheltenham so a bit quieter. Sleeps 2 Price from £130pn.

Tidmarton Mews
22 Malden Road, Cheltenham.
GL52 2BU.
Telephone: 01242 248177
Website: www.cheltenhamshortbreaks.
co.uk/tidmarton-mews/

Two bedroom mews house very close to the racecourse and Pittville Park. Sleeps 4 - 6.

Camping/Caravanning/Tourers

Cheltenham Caravan Club site
Prestbury Park, Cheltenham. GL50 4SH.
Telephone: 01242 523102
Website: www.caravanclub.co.uk

Open 05/04/2013 to 21/10/2013 - non caravan club members will have to pay a supplement.
If you are a train enthusiast and are planning a trip on the Honeybourne line (see things to do in Cheltenham) then this is the perfect spot.

Briarfields Touring Park
Gloucester Road, Off Cheltenham Road,
Cheltenham. GL51 0SX
Telephone: 01242 235324
Website: www.briarfields.net
Contact: Scott & Jo Sanderson

Open all year.

Gloucester - Places to Stay

Hotels & Inns

The New County Hotel

44 Southgate St, Gloucester. GL1 2DR
Telephone: 01452 307000
Website: www.thenewcountyhotel.co.uk

Slap bang (almost) in the Centre of Gloucester (a few doors down from the Tourist Information Centre) the New County Hotel has just been refurbished and is perfect to use a base to explore Gloucester itself or to use as a base for travels further afield. Very friendly team as well. Double rooms from £90 per night.

The Royal George Hotel

Birdlip, Gloucester. GL4 8JH.
Telephone: 01452 862506
Website: www.oldenglishinns.co.uk/birdlip/

Express by Holiday Inn - Gloucester

Telford Way, Gloucester. GL2 2AB
Telephone: 0870 720 0953

Just off the M5 Junction 12 so out of town. Contact the manager prior to booking if you are planning on taking your dog as there are some restrictions.

Hatherley Manor Hotel

Hatherley Manor, Down Hatherley Lane, Gloucester. GL2 9QA
Telephone: 01452 730217
Website: www.hatherleymanor.com

Rooms from £65 per night with a supplement of £10.00 per dog per night.

Ibis Hotel
Sawmills End, Corinium Ave,
Gloucester. GL4 3DG
Website: www.ibishotel.com

Budget hotel on the outskirts of Gloucester. Rooms from £35 per night. Book online only

Hatton Court Hotel
Upton Hill, Upton St. Leonards,
Gloucestershire. GL4 8DE
Telephone: 01452 617412
Website: www.hatton-court.co.uk

Part of the Hatton Court group that includes the White Hart in Winchcome and the Snooty Fox in Tetbury. Rooms from £65.

B&B

Longford Lodge Guest House
68 Tewkesbury Road, Gloucester.
GL2 9EH
Telephone: 01452 522243
Website: www.longfordlodge.co.uk
Contact: Jens Eberhardt

Rooms from £35 per night.

Self Catering

Hill Farm Cottages
Hill Farm, Upton St Leonards,
Gloucestershire. GL4 8DA
Telephone: 01452 614081
Contact: Mrs M McLellan

Two cottages sleeping 4 people. From £230 per week.

Hill Farm Barn

Birdlip Hill, Witcombe, Birdlip,
Gloucestershire. GL3 4SL
Telephone: 01452 864213
Website: www.cotswoldshortbreaks.
co.uk

Has a secure run so you can leave your
dog if you want to go out for the day. No
extra charge for dogs but bring your own
feeding bowls & bedding. Sleeps 4. Prices from £685.

Old Farm Cottages (2 cottages)

Barrel Lane, Longhope, Gloucestershire.
GL17 0LR
Telephone: 01452 830252
Website: www.oldfarmcottages.co.uk

Eggleton Strye - sleeps 5/6. From £296.
Sweet Coppins - sleeps 2/3. From £345.
Close to the Mayhill viewpoint, on a
working farm.

Camping/Caravanning/Tourers

The Hawbridge Inn

Haw Bridge, Tirley, Gloucester,
Gloucestershire. GL19 4HJ
Telephone: 01452 780316
Website: www.hawbridgeinn.co.uk

Campsite with toilet block and electric
hook up. Can take up to 10 caravans.

That's not flying, that's falling with style.

We were having a new bathroom fitted and the builders recommended that we moved out for a week, so we went to stay in Whitminster. There are plenty of walks nearby and it was so lovely to be able to take Skatie off the lead and let her run, as we could see everything around us for miles.

She was just full of the joys of spring and running like mad, when she jumped over a bit of low scrub, only to discover (too late) that there was a drop the other side. She sailed straight over, looked briefly shocked at the lack of ground beneath her and landed face first on a gravel path. We both ran over to her, and once we established that she wasn't badly hurt, burst into fits of giggles - which she joined in with in the way dogs do, barking and jumping around as if to say 'I've been funny haven't I?'

We usually have doggy tea tree ointment so we popped back to the cottage, washed the graze and picked out the bits of gravel then put plenty on. Like any lurcher worth their salt - she milked it for all she was worth…

We moved back home after a week to find that the great progress the builders had made on day one (ripping out the bathroom completely) was in fact the only progress they'd made. It took 9 weeks to finish. I never want to see a portable toilet again.

Stroud & Area - Places to Stay

Hotels & Inns

Amberley Inn

Culver Hill, Amberley, Stroud,
Gloucestershire. GL5 5AF
Telephone: 01453 872565
Website: www.theamberleyinn.co.uk

Resident dog Peggy welcomes you to the Amberley Inn (have a look at their entry in things to do for the story of how they ended up there). Standard rooms from £115 based on 2 sharing and a £10 a night supplement for dogs. Check out the website for special deals and weekend breaks.

The Ragged Cot Inn

Cirencester Road, Minchinhampton,
Gloucestershire. GL6 8PE
Telephone: 01453 884643
Website: www.theraggedcot.co.uk

This is an absolute jewel - the rooms are all named after famous penguin books - a real boutique style place. Sheepskin dog baskets are available for just £5 and they pass all proceeds to the Dogs Trust. Room prices include breakfast and start from £75 a night mid week.

The Bear of Rodborough

Rodborough Common, Stroud, Gloucestershire. GL5 5DE
Telephone: 01453 878522
Website: www.cotswold-inns-hotels.
co.uk/property/the_bear_of_rodborough

Dogs allowed in the accommodation with a charge of £10 per night. Must be kept on a lead in public areas and a rubber feeding mat is provided. Please let the management know in advance if you are bringing your pet as there are limited rooms available for dog owners. From £79 per person per night.

Burleigh Court Hotel

Burleigh, Minchinhampton,
Gloucestershire. GL5 2PF
Telephone: 01453 883804
Website: www.burleighcourthotel.co.uk

Dogs allowed in the standard coach house rooms only with an additional charge of £10 per night. From £140.

The Old Lodge

Minchinhampton Common, Stroud,
Gloucestershire. GL6 9AQ
Telephone: 01453 832047
Website: www.food-club.com/old-lodge.
htm
Twitter: @Nick_and_Chris

Boutique accommodation, all doubles with en-suite. Prices start from £70, No extra charge for dogs.

The Falcon

New Street, Painswick, Gloucestershire.
GL6 6UN
Telephone: 01452 813377
Website: www.falconpainswick.co.uk

Twelve bedrooms. Prices start from £75 for a double room. The Falcon is also a dog friendly gastro style pub.

The Old Crown Inn

17 The Green, Uley, Dursley,
Gloucestershire. GL11 5SN
Telephone: 01453 860502
Website: www.theoldcrownuley.co.uk

Has one room that's dog friendly - £70 per room per night.

The Crown Inn

Frampton Mansell, near Cirencester,
Gloucestershire. Gl6 8JG
Telephone: 01285 760601
Website: www.thecrowninn-cotswolds.
co.uk

Hotel annexe is separate from the pub. Rooms from £90 per night plus £5 per night doggy supplement.

Stonehouse Court Hotel

Bristol Rd, Stonehouse, Gloucestershire.
GL10 3RA
Telephone: 01453 794950
Website: www.stonehousecourt.co.uk

Easy access to canal walks from the hotel gardens. Rooms start from around £100 based on 2 people sharing and an additional £20 a night supplement is charged for dogs.

Swan Hotel

16 Market Street, Wotton-Under-Edge, Gloucestershire. GL12 7AE
Telephone: 01453 843004
Website: www.swanhotel.biz

£10 a night extra for dogs. Prices start from £75 per night.

B&B

Aaron Farm, Stroud

Nympsfield Road, Forest Green, Stroud, Gloucestershire. GL6 0ET
Telephone: 01453 833598
Website: None

Single rooms from £50, Doubles from £100.

Hyde Crest

Cirencester Road, Minchinhampton, Gloucestershire. GL6 8PE
Telephone: 01453 731631
Website: www.hydecrest.co.uk

One mile away from Minchinhampton Village. Pets by arrangement. Opposite the Ragged Cot pub. £70 per room per night. Strictly non-smokers.

The Laurels at Inchbrook

Inchbrook, Nailsworth, Gloucestershire. GL5 5HA
Telephone: 01453 834021
Website: www.SmoothHound.co.uk/hotels/thelaure.html

Five bedrooms on the 1st & 2nd floor and a cottage annexe with a further three bedrooms, including a ground floor room with wheelchair access and full disabled facilities. From £65 per night per room with reductions for longer stays. No extra charge for dogs.

Tibbiwell Lodge

Tibbiwell Lane Painswick, Gloucestershire. GL6 6YA
Telephone: 01452 812748
Website: www.tibbiwelllodgepainswick.webs.com

Dogs by special application - please contact for details. Rooms from £65.

Troy House Bed and Breakfast

Gloucester Street, Painswick, Gloucestershire. GL6 6QN
Telephone: 01452 812339
Website: www.troy-house.co.uk

£70 per room based on 2 sharing. English & Continental breakfasts available.

Viner House

24 Middle Street, Stroud, Gloucestershire. GL5 1DZ
Telephone: 01453 753949
Website: www.vinerhousestroud.co.uk

Double en-suite rooms from £55.00. Evening meals available by request.

The Withyholt Guest House

Stroud, Gloucestershire.
Telephone: 01452 813618
Website: www.thewithyholtbedandbreakfast.com
Contact: Mrs Peacey

There is a separate flat available for people who wish to visit with pets. Prices from £70 per night based on 2 people sharing.

Self Catering

The Coach House
Edgecombe House, Toadsmoor Road,
Brimscombe, Stroud, Gloucestershire.
GL5 2UG
Telephone: 01453 883147
Website: www.doggybreaks.co.uk

From £150 - £760. Sleeps 1-6. Has a
swimming pool and a hot tub. Website
states "Owners by arrangement".

Port House
London Road, Brimscombe, Stroud,
Gloucestershire. GL5 2QF
Telephone: 07765 644016
Website: www.port-house.co.uk
Contact: Jane Green

Sleeps 7 guests in three bedrooms. From
£448 per week.

Port House Apartment
London Road, Brimscombe, Stroud,
Gloucestershire. GL5 2QF
Telephone: 07765 644016
Website: www.port-house.co.uk
Contact: Jane Green

Sleeps 2 in one bedroom - from £48 per
night or £294 per week.

Tibbiwell Lodge
Tibbiwell Lane Painswick,
Gloucestershire. GL6 6YA
Telephone: 01452 812748
Website: www.tibbiwelllodgepainswick.
webs.com

Tibbiwell Lodge also have a self catering
apartment. Dogs by special application
- please contact for details. Price from
£450 pw. Sleeps up to 4.

Broadridge Mews
Buckholt road, Cranham,
Gloucestershire. Gl4 8HF
Telephone: 01452 863011
Website: www.holidaycheltenham.co.uk
Contact: Tom and Helen Daltry

Close to one of our favourite walks in
Cranham Woods.

Sleeps 4 (1 double, 1 sofa bed) Prices
from £250 pw.

Whitminster Cottages

Telephone: 01452 740204
Website: www.whitminsterhousecot-
tages.co.uk

A cluster of holiday cottages, all but two
(West Wing & Old Stables) allow dogs at
£15 per week.
Walk Farmhouse - Sleeps 11 from £899.
Walk House - Sleeps 9 from £729.
Walk Close - Sleeps 3 (level access) from
£379.
Walk Farm Cottage - Sleeps 3 + d s/b
from £379.
All four together sleep 26 - 30 people.
Lodge Cottage - Sleeps 4 from £459.
Church Cottage - Sleeps 7 from £659.

Stable Cottage

Oakridge, Stroud, Gloucestershire.
Telephone 01452 770407
Website: www.fivevalleyscottages.co.uk
Contact: Antony Newman

Sleeps 1 - 4 cost £275 - £495 per week.
Shared swimming pool. Vegetables, eggs
& lamb are available to purchase from the
farm depending on the season.

Bell House Apartment

Wallbridge Lock, Stroud
Telephone: 07765 644016
Website: www.port-house.co.uk
Contact: Jane Green

Two apartments. Apartment one sleeps 5
in 2 bedrooms, Apartment 2 sleeps 4 in
two bedrooms, from £455 per week.

Sawmills Cottage Ebley

Telephone: 07765 644016
Website: www.port-house.co.uk
Contact Jane Green

One bedroom cottage sleeps 2. From
£294 per week.

The Old Mill

Oakridge Lynch, Gloucestershire.
GL6 7NY
Telephone: 01242 248177
Website: www.cotswoldcottagesonline.
com/the-old-mill

Sleeps 20. Prices from £4000 per week.

Blandfords
Oakridge Lynch, Gloucestershire.
GL6 7NY
Telephone: 01242 248177
Website: www.cotswoldcottagesonline.
com/blandfords

Sleeps 10. Prices from £1550 per week.

Camping/Caravanning/Tourers

Hogsdown Farm Camping Site
Wotton Road, Dursley. Gloucestershire.
GL11 6DS
Telephone: 01453 810224
Website: www.hogsdownfarm.co.uk

Dogs must be kept on a lead and walked off the park.

Tudor Caravan Park
Shepherds Patch, Slimbridge,
Gloucestershire. GL2 7BP
Telephone: 01453 890483
Website: www.tudorcaravanpark.com

Open all year.

Absolutely slap bang next to the Gloucester and Sharpness canal so plenty of walks/cycling/fishing along the canal path. Has the dog friendly Tudor Arms next door.

Adults only area as well as family camping.

Apple Tree Park
A38 Claypits, Stonehouse, Stroud,
Gloucestershire. GL10 3AL
Telephone: 01452 742362
Website: www.appletreepark.co.uk
Contact: John Stayte

Open all year.

South Cotswolds - Places to Stay

Hotels & Inns

The Fleece Hotel
Market Place, Cirencester,
Gloucestershire, GL7 2NZ
Telephone: 01285 658507
Website: www.thefleececirencester.co.uk

Rooms from £99.00. Dogs can be left in bedrooms unattended and have access to lounge only, exercise area is 100mtrs away.

Corinium Hotel
12 Gloucester Street, Cirencester,
Gloucestershire. GL7 2DG
Telephone: 01285 659711
Website: www.coriniumhotel.com
Contact: Tim and Carol Waller

Double occupancy from £95. Have one dog friendly room.

Best Western Stratton House Hotel
Gloucester road, Cirencester,
Gloucestershire. GL7 2LE
Telephone: 01285 651761
Website: www.strattonhousehotel.com

Prices vary, however dogs are charged at £7.50 per dog per night.

The Crown Of Crucis
Ampney Crucis, Cirencester,
Gloucestershire. GL7 5RS
Telephone: 01285 851806
Website: www.thecrownofcrucis.co.uk

The Crown Inn Frampton Mansell

Frampton Mansell, near Cirencester, Gloucestershire. GL6 8JG
Telephone: 01285 760601
Website: www.thecrowninn-cotswolds.co.uk

£87.50 per night. Dogs £5 per night.

The Bibury Court Hotel

Bibury, Cirencester, Gloucestershire. GL7 5NT
Telephone: 01285 740337
Website: www.biburycourt.co.uk

Up to two dogs allowed per room at a charge of £10 per dog per night. Dogs not allowed in public areas of the hotel.

The Puesdown Inn

Compton Abdale, Cheltenham, Gloucestershire. GL54 4DN
Telephone: 01451 860262
Website: www.puesdown.cotswoldinns.com

The Puesdown Inn is brilliantly situated on the A40 plonking it almost in the middle of more places to explore than you can shake a stick at! Dogs are allowed in the bar area and soft areas but must be kept on a lead and under control. Dogs are not allowed to be left in rooms unattended. Price from £75 per night.

The Wheatsheaf Inn

West end, Northleach, Gloucestershire. GL54 3EZ
Telephone: 01451 860244
Website: www.cotswoldswheatsheaf.com
Twitter: @WheatsheafGL54

Listed in the Alistair Sawday and Mr & Mrs Smith guide.
Gorgeous luxury Inn. There are 3 rooms where you can stay with your dog (usual rules apply). Fantastic food here. Rooms from £120 per night with a doggy surcharge of £10 per dog per night (up to a maximum of 2 dogs).

The Sherbourne Arms

Market Place, Northleach, Gloucestershire. GL54 3EE
Telephone: 01451 860241

Rooms from £50 per night. Pets by arrangement.

The Inn at Fossebridge

Fossebridge, Fosseway, Cheltenham,
Gloucestershire. GL54 3JS
Telephone: 01285 720721
Website: www.cotswolds-country-pub-
hotel.co.uk
Twitter: @FossebridgeInn

Accept well behaved dogs in the hotel rooms and all public areas of the Inn with an additional charge of £15 per night. Rooms from £125 per night.

The Hunters Hall Inn

Kingscote, Nr. Tetbury, Gloucestershire.
GL8 8XZ
Telephone: 01453 860393
Website: www.oldenglishinns.co.uk/
kingscote/index.php

Rooms from £70

The Snooty Fox

Market Place, Tetbury, Gloucestershire.
GL8 8DD
Telephone. 01666 502436
Website: www.snooty-fox.co.uk

Doubles from £80 or you could splash out (sorry) on a four poster room with a whirlpool bath from £210. Home to George the great dane.

The Hare & Hounds Tetbury

Westonbirt, Tetbury, Gloucestershire.
GL8 8Q
Telephone: 01666 881000
Website: www.cotswold-inns-hotels.
co.uk/property/hare_and_hounds_hotel/
index.htm

Dogs allowed in the accommodation with a charge of £10 per night. Must be kept on a lead in public areas and a rubber feeding mat is provided. Please let the manage- ment know in advance if you are bringing your pet as there are limited rooms avail- able for dog owners. From £79 per person per night. Useful dog walking map down- loadable from their website.

Self Catering

Hartwell Farm Cottages

Ready Token, nr. Bibury, Cirencester,
Gloucestershire. Gl7 5Sy
Telephone: 01285 740210
Website: www.selfcateringcotswolds.
com
Contact: Mrs Mann

Two self catering cottages. Lilac sleeps
3 (plus cot and extra folding bed) and
Lavendar sleeps 4 (plus extra cot/folding
bed). Mid season prices around £425.

Lakeland Cottage

Fossebridge, Fosseway, Cheltenham,
Gloucestershire. GL54 3JS
Telephone: 01285 720721
Website: www.cotswolds-country-pub-
hotel.co.uk
Twitter: @FossebridgeInn

In the grounds of The Inn at Fossebridge.

Sleeps up to 10 people in 4 bedrooms.
Additional £15 per dog per night (bed &
bowl provided!) From £1,250 per week.

Camping/Caravanning/Tourers

Cirencester Park Caravan Club Site

Stroud Road, Cirencester,
Gloucestershire. GL7 1UT
Telephone: 01285 651546

Opening dates 22/03/2013 to 04/01/2014.

Mayfield Park

Cheltenham Road, Perrotts Brook,
Cirencester, Gloucestershire. GL7 7BH
Telephone: 01285 831301
Website: www.mayfieldpark.co.uk

Open all year.

The Tunnel House Inn

Tarlton Road, Nr Cirencester,
Gloucestershire. GL7 6PW
Telephone: 01285 770280
Website: www.tunnelhouse.com

This is one of Skateboard's approved eateries and they have started to allow camping in the grounds.

Far Peak Campsite

Far Peak, Northleach, Gloucestershire.
GL54 3JL
Telephone: 01285 720858
Website: www.farpeakcamping.co.uk

Open April to October.

The Daneway Inn

Daneway, Cirencester, GL7 6LN
Telephone: 01285 760297
Website: www.thedaneway.com

Open from Easter.

North Cotswolds - Places to Stay

Covers:

Bourton-on-the-Water/The Slaughters/The Rissingtons, Burford, Chipping Campden, Morton-in-Marsh, Stow-on-the-Wold

Hotels & Inns

Chester House Hotel

Victoria Street, Bourton-on-the-Water, Gloucestershire. GL54 2BU
Telephone: 01451 820286
Website: www.chesterhousehotel.com
Twitter: @chesterHHotel

Twenty two bedroom centrally located hotel. Prices from £90 per room per night. It is possible to book beauty treatments in your room.

Dial House Hotel & Restaurant

Station Road, Bourton-on-the-Water, Gloucestershire. GL54 2AA
Telephone: 01451 822244
Website: www.dialhousehotel.com

Has a selection of dog friendly rooms. £10 per night charge for dogs. Rooms from £99 (also check the website for special offers and breaks).

The Duke of Wellington

Sherbourne Street, Bourton-on-the-water, Gloucestershire. GL54 2BY
Telephone: 01451 820539
Website: www.dukeofwellingtonbourton. co.uk

Dog friendly accommodation - please advise at the time of booking that you are bringing a dog - the owners like to keep some rooms free of animal hair etc for other guests who may have any problematic conditions.
Rooms from £80.00 per night - contact them for any special offers. Double and twin rooms.

The Bull at Burford,

105 High Street, Burford, Oxfordshire.
OX18 4RG.
Telephone: 01993 822220
Website: www.bullatburford.co.uk

Rooms from £70. Pets by arrangement.

The Burford Lodge

Oxford Road, Burford, Oxfordshire. OX18
4PH
Telephone: 01993 823354
Website: www.burfordlodge.com

Rooms from £90 per night on a B&B basis.

Dogs charged at £7.50 per night and must not be left alone in the room.

Cotswold Gateway Hotel

216, The Hill, Burford, Oxfordshire. OX18
4HX
Telephone: 01993 822695
Website: www.cotswold-gateway.co.uk

Pets are allowed at no extra charge but please confirm in advance.

Rooms from £65 per night on a B&B basis.

The Highway Inn

117 High Street, Burford, Oxfordshire.
OX18 4RG
Telephone: 01993 823661
Website: www.thehighwayhotel.co.uk

Welcome dogs but it is best to give them a call to check sizes!

Rooms from £89 with full breakfast.

The Royal Oak

26 Witney Street, Burford, Oxfordshire.
OX18 4SN
Telephone: 01993 823278
Website: www.royaloakburford.co.uk

Double or twin room from £80 per night.

The Lamb Inn

Sheep Street, Burford, Oxfordshire.
OX18 4LR
Telephone: 01993 823155
Website: www.cotswold-inns-hotels.co.uk/
property/the_lamb_inn?/lamb

From £80 per person per night.

The Bay Tree Hotel

Sheep Street, Burford, Oxfordshire.
OX18 4LW
Telephone: 01993 822 791
Website: www.cotswold-inns-hotels.co.uk/
property/the_bay_tree_hotel

From £85 per person per night. Pets allowed on request - no extra charge.

Inn for all Seasons

The Barringtons, Nr Burford,Oxfordshire.
OX18 4TN
Telephone: 01451 844324
Website: www.innforallseasons.com

Dogs can be left in bedrooms unattended and can go anywhere in the hotel, including the bar /informal eating area. Dogs are not allowed in the restaurant. Access to open fields to the rear of the hotel & lovely walks.
Resident pets are Bob Sharp (Black Labrador) & Ted Sharp (Black German Shepherd). Rooms from £95.00.

The Fox Inn Barrington

Great Barrington, Oxfordshire. OX18 4TB
Telephone: 01451 844385
Website: www.foxinnbarrington.com

Two dog friendly rooms as well as a room with a friendly ghost. Rooms from £60.

Charingworth Manor

Charingworth, Nr Chipping Campden,
Gloucestershire. GL55 6NS
Telephone: 01386 593555
Website: www.classiclodges.co.uk/Charingworth_Manor_The_Cotswolds

Welcomes well behaved dogs. Rooms from £145.

Lygon Arms Hotel

High Street, Chipping Campden,
Gloucestershire. GL55 6HB
Telephone: 01386 840318
Website: www.lygonarms.co.uk

Do have some dog friendly rooms but must be booked in advance. £110 - £160 based on 2 people sharing.

The Red Lion Inn

High Street, Chipping Camden,
Gloucestershire. GL55 6AS
Telephone: 01386 840760
Website: www.theredlioninn.org

B&B Accommodation from £65 for a smaller double.

The Noel Arms Hotel

High Street, Chipping Campden,
Gloucestershire. GL55 6AT
Telephone: 01386 840317
Website: www.noelarmshotel.com
Twitter: @noelarms

Dogs are welcome and are charged at £15 per stay. Prices from £90 per room per night on a B&B basis. Guests who are staying with dogs can dine in either the bar or the conservatory.

Threeways House

Mickleton, Chipping Campden,
Gloucestershire. Gl55 6SB
Telephone: 01386 438429
Website: www.threewayshousehotel.com or www.puddingclub.com
Twitter: @ThreeWaysHouse
Contact: Jill Coombe

The home of the famous pudding club, well behaved dogs are welcome at the Three Ways House hotel. Rooms from £145. Runs a number of walking weekends throughout the year.

Cotswold House Hotel and Spa

The Square, Chipping Campden,
Gloucestershire. GL55 6AN
Telephone: 01386 840330
Website: www.cotswoldhouse.com
Twitter: @cotswoldhousegl

Dogs are allowed to stay in the cottage rooms at a charge of £25 per night.

The Bell Inn

High Street, Morton-in-Marsh,
Gloucestershire. GL56 0AF.
Telephone. 01608 651688
Website: www.thebellatmoreton.co.uk

En-suite guest accommodation in the guest houses in the courtyard and also the stable block at the front of the pub. Rooms from £90 per night.

The Manor House Hotel

High Street, Morton-in-Marsh,
Gloucestershire. GL56 OLJ
Telephone: 01608 650 501
Website: www.cotswold-inns-hotels.co.uk/
property/the_manor_house_hotel/

Rooms from £79. Dogs £10 per dog
per night.

White Hart Royal Hotel

High St, Morton-in-Marsh,
Gloucestershire. GL56 0BA
Telephone: 01608 650731
Website: www.whitehartroyal.co.uk
Twitter: @Whitehartroyal

Three rooms allocated for dogs, 2 of
which have garden spaces. Everywhere open for dogs except the restaurant. Rooms from £130.

Red Lion Little Compton

Little Compton, Morton-in-Marsh,
Gloucestershire. GL56 0RT
Telephone: 01608 674397
Website: www.theredlionlittlecompton.
co.uk

Prices from £75 per room per night (although do have some special offers on
the website). Doggy surcharge of £5
per dog and please do let them know
that you are bringing a dog when you
book.

The Crown Hotel

High Street Blockley, Moreton-in-Marsh,
Gloucestershire. GL56 9EX
Telephone: 01386 700245
Website: www.crownhotelblockley.co.uk

Double rooms from £85 per night.
Dogs allowed by prior arrangement.

The Golden Ball Inn

Lower Swell, Gloucestershire. GL54 1LF
Telephone: 01451 833886
Website: www.thegoldenballinn.com

One double ensuite B&B room where
'well behaved guests can stay with
their dogs'. Rates are on the website
and start from £65.00.

The Old Stocks Hotel

The Square, Stow-on-the-Wold,
Gloucestershire. GL54 1AF
Telephone: 01451 830666
Website: www.oldstockshotel.co.uk

Rooms from £65 (DBB) Additional charge of £5 per dog

The Kings Arms

Market Square, Stow-on-the-Wold,
Gloucestershire. GL54 1AF
Telephone: 01451 830364
Website: www.kingsarmsstow.co.uk
Twitter: @kingsarmsstow

The Grapevine

Sheep Street, Stow-on-the-Wold,
Gloucestershire. GL54 1AU
Telephone: 01451 830344
Website: www.thegrapevinehotel.com

Rooms from £125 B&B. Opposite the Royalist Hotel & Eagle and Child.

The Royalist Hotel

Digbeth Street, Stow-on-the-Wold,
Gloucestershire. GL54 1BN
Telephone: 01451 830670
Website: www.theroyalisthotel.com

Rooms from £125 B&B. Food served at the Eagle & Child next door.

B&B

Fieldways B&B

Chapel Lane, Cold Aston,
Bourton-on-the-Water, Gloucestershire.
GL54 3BJ
Telephone: 01451 810659
Website: www.fieldways.com
Contact: Alan Graham

One double room and two twin rooms.
Prices start from £95.00. Boutique B&B
that features in Sawdays Special Places to
Stay. Well behaved dogs accepted.

Over the Bridge B&B

4 Letch Hill Drive,
Bourton-on-the-Water, Gloucestershire.
GL54 2DQ.
Telephone: 01451 820171
Website: www.overthebridgebourton.
co.uk
Contact: Paula Glyn

One double family room has its own entrance with a lounge area, TV & Tea/cof-
fee making facilities. Prices from £70 including breakfast. Please bring your dogs
own bedding, no extra charge for dogs.

Halford House

Station Road, Bourton-on-the-Water,
Gloucestershire. GL54 2AA
Telephone: 01451 822244
Website: www.halfordhouse.com
Contact: Elaine Booth

The Garden Room Strathspey

Lansdowne, Bourton-on-the-Water,
Gloucestershire. GL54 2AR
Telephone: 01451 810321
Website: www.strathspeybandb.co.uk
Contact: Emma & John

From £60 per day - accepts one small dog
at £5 per night.

Southlands B&B

Rissington road, Bourton-on-the-Water, Gloucestershire. Gl54 2DT
Telephone: 01451 821987
Website: www.southlands-bb.co.uk

From £75 per night for a double room.

Holly House Bed & Breakfast

Ebrington, Chipping Campden, Gloucestershire. GL55 6NL
Telephone: 01386 593213
Website: www.hollyhousebandb.co.uk
Contact: Jeffrey Hutsby

From £70 per room per night based on 2 people sharing, Holly house is just 2 miles from Chipping Campden. Please note that Holly House don't accept debit or credit cards. Not far from the Ebrington Arms which is a dog friendly pub.

The Court B&B

Calf Lane, Chipping Campden, Gloucestershire. GL55 6JQ
Telephone: 01386 840201
Website: www.thecourtchippingcampden.co.uk
Contact: Jane

Rooms from £50. Quiet well behaved dogs are welcome.

1 The Old Manor

Paxford, Chipping Campden, Gloucestershire. GL55 6XL
Telephone: 01386 593130
Website: www.oldmanorpaxford.com
Contact: Rob & Jan Kirton

Had a lovely chat with Jan on the phone - she's lovely! Dogs are welcome by arrangement so best to phone and chat through your requirements. From £65 per night and no additional charge for dogs.

Guiting Guest House

Post Office Lane, Guiting Power, Gloucestershire. Gl54 5TZ
Telephone: 01451 850470
Website: www.guitingguesthouse.com
Contact: Barbara Millar

Dogs are accepted in allocated rooms with prior notice. The guest house also has self catering accommodation. Prices from £78.

Fosseway Farm B&B (also a campsite)

Stow Road, Morton-in-Marsh,
Gloucestershire. GL56 0DS
Telephone: 01608 650503
Website: www.fossewayfarm.co.uk

One downstairs room allocated for dogs,
prices from £95.

Jasmine Cottage

Balcony Lane, Stretton-on-Fosse, Nr
Morton-in-Marsh, Gloucestershire.
GL56 9SA
Telephone: 01608 661972
Website: www.jasminecottagebandb.
co.uk

Doubles from £60 per night.

Acacia

2 New Road, Morton-in-Marsh,
Gloucestershire. GL56 0AS.
Telephone: 01608 650130
Website: www.acaciabedandbreakfast.
co.uk

Chapel House B&B

3-4 Chapel Row, Little Compton near
Moreton-in-Marsh, Gloucestershire.
GL56 0RX
Telephone: 01608 674367
Website: www.chapelhousebedandbreak-
fast.co.uk

£65.00 and £5.00 for dog. Very dog
friendly accommodation (2 dogs only
please). The cottage is two knocked into
one so guest rooms are totally private

Self Catering

Southlands

Rissington road, Bourton-on-the-Water, Gloucestershire. Gl54 2DT
Telephone: 01451 821987
Website: www.southlands-bb.co.uk

A wheelchair accessible 3 bedroom cottage in the grounds of the B&B. One small dog welcome. From £590 per week.

Noel Cottage

Chipping Campden, Gloucestershire.
Telephone: 01386 840835
Website: www.cotswoldcottages.uk.com/noel.htm

£275 - £500 per week. Sleeps: 1 to 2.

Cider Mill Cottage

Chipping Campden, Gloucestershire.
Telephone: 01386 593315
Website: www.campdencottages.co.uk/search/CiderMillCottageChippingCampden.htm

One small dog permitted by prior arrangement. From £410 - £655 per week.

Peacocks Cottage

Fifield, Chipping Norton, Gloucestershire.
Telephone: 01993 830484
Website: www.rosemaryscottages.co.uk/thecottage-p.html

£295 - £475 per week Sleeps: 1 to 5. One double bedroom and one twin.

Cinquefoil Cottage

54 Park Road, Blockley, Gloucestershire. GL56 9BZ
Telephone: 01707 652485
Website: www.cinquefoilcottage.co.uk

Sleeps up to 4 in one double and one twin. Prices from £200 - £380 per week depending on season. Dogs permitted by arrangement at £5 per week.

The Cottage
Henmarsh House, Moreton-in-Marsh,
Gloucestershire. GL56 0PJ
Telephone: 01608 674601.
Website www.webcottages.co.uk/thecottageathenmarshhouse
Contact: Ms Suzie Coker.

Sleeps 2 - 5. Prices from £295 - £550pw.
Well behaved dogs welcome.
The property is next to a bridle path so you can quite simply open the gate and start walking. Two double bedrooms (one on the ground floor) and one single.

Rosemary Cottage
Blockley, Moreton-in-Marsh,
Gloucestershire.
Telephone: 01386 593315
Website: www.campdencottages.co.uk/
properties/rosemary_cottage.htm

Sleeps 4 people (children over 5). From £395 per week. Dogs welcome by arrangement but need to stay downstairs. Close to Great Western Arms pub (which is super doggy friendly).

Rockbank Cottage
Blockley, Moreton-in-Marsh,
Gloucestershire.
Telephone: 01386 593315
Website: www.campdencottages.co.uk/
properties/rockbank_cottage.htm

Sleeps 1 - 6. £520 - £815 per week.

Luckley Farm Cottages
Longborough, Moreton-in-Marsh,
Gloucestershire.
Telephone: 01451 870885
Website: www.luckley-holidays.co.uk/
cottages.php

Sleeps 1 - 32. £300 - £2200 per week. Two barns, the Granary sleeps 1 - 12+ and the Warren sleeps 1 - 18.

Blackpitt Farm Cottages
Stow-on-the-Wold, Cotswolds,
Gloucestershire.
Telephone: 01451 831855
Website: www.blackpitt.co.uk

Stable cottage sleeps 4 - 5 people and costs from £275 a week.

Well cottage sleeps 2 and costs from £250 a week.

The Kings Arms
Market Square, Stow-on-the-Wold,
Gloucestershire. GL54 1AF
Telephone: 01451 830364
Website: www.kingsarmsstow.co.uk
Twitter: @kingsarmsstow

Three Cottages to the rear of the Kings Arms - all sleep 2 in one double.

Bibury
Condicote, Nr Stow-on-the-Wold,
Gloucestershire. GL54 1ER
Telephone: 01451 832215
Website: www.cotswoldfarmhouse.com

Five spacious converted barns sleeping between 2 and 14 people. Prices from £490 - £2250 per week.
Games room with snooker & table tennis, hard tennis court & badminton. 1 well behaved dog over 18 months old.

The Granary
Wren House, Donnington, Stow-on-the-Wold, Gloucestershire. GL56 0XZ
Telephone: 01451 831787
Website: www.wrenhouse.net/self-catering-cottage

One Bed Cottage. Dogs allowed but not upstairs. Plenty of information about local eateries (not all dog friendly) on the website. Prices from £455-£750 per week.

Camping/Caravanning/Tourers

Field Barn Park
Bourton-on-the-water, Cheltenham,
Gloucestershire. GL54 2LF
Telephone: 01451 820 434
Website: www.fieldbarnpark.com
Contact: Martin MacCurrach

Open April - September. Adults only (Aged 30+) Downloadable directions on the website.

163

Folly Farm Cotswold Camping

Bourton-on-the-Water, Gloucestershire.
GL54 3BY
Telephone: 01451 820 285
Website: www.cotswoldcamping.net

Open March to October.

Two footpaths connect to the Gloucester way.

Cotswold Carp Farm

Bury Barn, Bourton-on-the-Water,
Gloucestershire. GL54 2HB
Telephone: 01451 821795

Open March to October – small exclusive site with fishing available for people camping. Accepts dogs but no children allowed. Book in advance.

Cotswold Farm Park

Guiting Power, Cheltenham,
Gloucestershire. GL54 5UG
Telephone: 01451 850307
Website: www.cotswoldfarmpark.co.uk
Twitter: @cotswoldfarmpk

Open: March to November

Run by Adam Henson whom we regularly see on Country File and Lambing Live. Dogs are allowed in the campsite but not in the park as it is a rare breeds farm. The campsite is pretty much central to Winchcombe/Moreton/Broadway and Bourton-on-the-Water so plenty of dog friendly things to do.

Moreton-in-Marsh Caravan Club Site

Bourton Road, Moreton-In-Marsh,
Gloucestershire. GL56 0BT
Telephone: 01608 650519
Website: www.caravanclub.co.uk

Open all year - non caravan club members will have to pay a supplement.

Fosseway Farm

Stow Road, Morton-in-Marsh,
Gloucestershire. GL56 0DS
Telephone: 01608 650503
Website: www.fossewayfarm.co.uk
Contact Sandra, Mo, Alf and John

Open all year.

Lemington Lakes Caravan Park

Todenham Road, Morton-in-Marsh, Gloucestershire. GL56 9NP
Telephone: 01608 650872
Website: www.lemingtonlakes.co.uk
Contact: Andy & Debbie

Open all year - one of the very few 'caravan only' sites we're listing but we thought we would include it as it is primarily a fishing holiday site (although the fishery is closed from 1st November to 28th February).

Appendices:

Emergency Numbers - Vets & Dog Wardens

We thought it would be useful to include details of dog wardens and vets with links wherever possible to websites.

I apologise in advance for some of the home spun websites featured here - one can only assume that a handful of vets seem to think that their ability to stitch stuff back on animals also makes them a master of the HTML. I'll leave you to draw your own conclusions.

Forest of Dean

Forest Of Dean Dog Warden 01594 812264. Out of hours number: 07505 820220. You can also report a lost dog to the street wardens who regularly patrol.

Severnside Veterinary Group

1 Tuthill, Lydney. GL15 5PA

Telephone 01594 842185

Website: www.severnsideveterinarygroup.co.uk

Drybridge Veterinary Clinic

Railway Drive, Coleford. GL16 8RH

Telephone 01594 833526

Website: www.drybridgevets.co.uk

Sundean Veterinary Clinic

9 - 11 High Street, Lydney. GL15 5DP

Telephone: 01594 840404

Website: www.sundeanvets.co.uk

Millpark Veterinary Centre

Cleeve Mill Business Park, Newent. GL18 1AZ

Telephone 01531 820528

Website: www.millparkvets.com

Petsbarn Veterinary Group

Heywood Road, Cinderford. GL14 2PL.

Telephone 01594 826688 Emergency cover 01452 830421

Website: www.petsbarn.co.uk

Petsbarn Veterinary Group

Harts Barn Farm, Longhope. GL17 0QD

Telephone 01594 830086 Emergency cover 01452 830421

Website: www.petsbarn.co.uk

The Globe Veterinary Surgery

115 High Street, Cinderford. GL14 2TB

Telephone 01594 824416

Website: None to date

Tewkesbury/Winchcombe/Broadway

Tewkesbury Dog Warden 01684 272191. Out of hours service 01684 293445

The Coldicott Veterinary Clinic

Barton Street, Tewkesbury. GL20 5PX

Telephone: 01684 292177

Website: www.coldicottvet.org.uk

Twitter: @ColdicottVet

Has interactive symptom guide on website.

The Crescent Veterinary Centre

31 Church St, Tewkesbury. GL20 5PD

Telephone 01684 290500

Website: None to date

Folly Gardens

1, Folly Gardens, Barton Road, Tewkesbury. GL20 5QP

Telephone: 01684 292244

Website: www.follygardens.com

Twitter: @tewkesburyvets

Chase Veterinary Clinic

Stone Acre, School Lane, Ripple, Tewkesbury. GL20 6EU

Telephone: 01684 593434

Website: None to date

Kearns & Rea

Stratford Bridge, Ripple, Tewkesbury. GL20 6HE

Telephone: 01684 592099

Website: None to date

Vets On The Park

12 Columbine Road, Walton Cardiff, Tewkesbury. GL20 7SP

Telephone: 01684 290 088

Website: www.vetsonthepark.co.uk

Abbey Green Veterinary Group

Abbey Cottage, Abbey Terrace, Winchcombe. GL54 5LW

Telephone: 01242 602235

Website: www.abbeygreenvets.co.uk

Abbey Green Veterinary Group

Church Close, Broadway, Worcestershire. WR12 7AH

Telephone: 01386 852421

Website: www.abbeygreenvets.co.uk

Cheltenham

Cheltenham Dog Warden 01242 264135 (ask to be put through to the dog warden) or via email dogwarden@cheltenham.gov.uk

Vets on the Park

Moorend Grove, Cheltenham. GL53 OEX

Telephone: 01242 517199

Website: www.vetsonthepark.co.uk

Dragon Veterinary Centre

New Barn Lane, Cheltenham. GL50 4SH

Telephone: 01242 580324

Website: www.dragonvet.co.uk

Folly Gardens

5, Church Road, Bishop's Cleeve, Cheltenham. GL52 8LR

Telephone: 01242 679880

Website: www.follygardens.com

Twitter: @tewkesburyvets

Honeybourne Veterinary Centre

Ferlys House, Overton Park Rd, Cheltenham. GL50 3BP

Telephone: 01242 522429

Website: www.honeybourne.com

MacDonald Veterinary Clinic

20 Cleevemount Road, Prestbury, Cheltenham. GL52 3HG

Telephone: 01242 260144

Website: www.macdonaldvets.co.uk

MacDonald Veterinary Clinic

Leckhampton hospital: 6 Bethesda Street, GL50 2AY

Telephone: 01242 234 392

Website: www.macdonaldvets.co.uk

Casvet

Gardner's Lane, Cheltenham. GL51 9JW

Telephone 01242 530056 (attached to Cheltenham Animal Shelter)

Website: www.gawa.org.uk

Arvonia Animal Hospital

The Reddings, Cheltenham. GL51 6RY

Telephone: 01242 700100

Website: www.cheltenhamvets.co.uk

Twitter: @arvoniavets

Woodlands Veterinary Clinic

Salisbury Avenue, Warden Hill, Cheltenham. GL51 3GA

Telephone: 01242 255133

Website: www.woodlands-vets.co.uk

Gloucester

Gloucester Dog Warden 01452 396396

Aspinall Auld & Stevenson

20 Glenvum Way, Abbeydale, Gloucester. GL4 4BL.

Telephone: 01452 300596

Website: www.aspinallauldstevensongl4.co.uk or www.aasvets.co.uk

Brambles Veterinary Surgery

58 Albermarle Road Churchdown, Gloucester. GL3 2HE

Telephone: 01452 712194

Website: www.brambles-vets.co.uk

Pets Barn Vet Centre & Animal Hospital

Hartpury, Gloucester. GL19 3BG

Telephone: 01452 700086 Emergency cover 01452 830421

Website: www.petsbarn.co.uk

Wood Veterinary Group

125 Bristol Road, Quedgeley, Gloucester. GL2 4NB

Telephone 01452 520056

Website: (and it's a bit of an eye bleeder - sorry) www.woodvet.co.uk

S.P.A. Vet Services Ltd

228 Painswick Rd, Gloucester. GL4 4PH

Telephone 01452 529480

Website: www.spa-vets.co.uk

Aspinall Auld & Stevenson (Now AAS Vets)

108 Bristol Rd, Quedgeley, Gloucester. GL2 4NA.

Telephone 01452 722089

Website: www.aasvets.co.uk

North Cotswolds

Cotswold Dog Warden 01285 623000

You can also report lost dogs online at their website: www.cotswold.gov.uk

Stow Veterinary Surgeons

Maugersbury Road, Stow-on-the-Wold. GL54 1HH

Telephone: 01451 830620

Website: www.stowvets.co.uk

Shipston Veterinary Centre Branch Surgery

Hospital Road, Moreton-in-Marsh. GL56 0BQ

Telephone: 01608 661232

Website: None to date

Stow Veterinary Surgeons

Old Market Way, Moreton-in-Marsh. GL56 0AJ

Telephone: 01451 830620

Website: www.stowvets.co.uk

South Cotswolds

Cotswold Dog Warden 01285 623000

You can also report lost dogs online at their website: www.cotswold.gov.uk

South Gloucestershire Dog Warden 01454 868000

The George Veterinary Group

23 Church Street, Tetbury. GL8 8JG

Telephone: 01666 503531

Website: www.georgevetgroup.co.uk

Ashcroft Veterinary Surgery

Cirencester Business Park, Elliott Rd, Love Lane, Cirencester. GL7 1YS

Telephone: 01285 653683

Website: www.ashcroftvets.org.uk

The Sidings Veterinary Surgery

Sheep St, Cirencester. GL7 1QW

Telephone: 01285 643146

Website: www.sidingsvets.co.uk

Benson & Babb

45 Lewis Lane, Cirencester. GL7 1EA

Telephone: 01285 656868 or 01285 653151

Website: www.bensonandbabb-cirencester.co.uk

Davies & Evans

The Bridge Veterinary Clinic, Milton Street, Fairford, Gloucestershire. GL7 4BW

Tel. 01285 713555

Stroud

Stroud Dog Warden 01453 754478

Bowbridge Veterinary Group

17 Gloucester Road, Stonehouse. GL10 2NZ

Telephone: 01453 825796 Emergency number is 01453 762350

Website: www.bowbridgevets.co.uk

Bowbridge Veterinary Group

Butterrow Hill, Stroud. GL5 2LA

Telephone: 01453 762350

Website: www.bowbridgevets.co.uk

Aspinall Auld & Stevenson, Stroud

Five Valleys Veterinary Practice, 130 Cainscross Rd, Stroud. GL5 4HN.

Telephone: 01453 765304

Website: www.aasvets.co.uk

Acorn Veterinary Clinic

Middle Hill Farm, Middle Hill, Chalford Hill, Stroud. GL6 8BE

Telephone: 01453 886984

Website: None to date

The Veterinary Clinic

Old Market Place, Nailsworth. GL6 0DU

Telephone: 01453 834930

Website: www.lansdownvets.co.uk

Lansdown Veterinary Surgeons

Clock House Veterinary Hospital, Wallbridge, Stroud. GL5 3JD

Telephone: 01453 752555

Website: www.lansdownvets.co.uk

Rowe Veterinary Group

Bradley Green, Wotton under Edge, Gloucestershire. GL12 7PP

Telephone: 01453 843295 (24 hours) Emergency Number: 01454 275000

Website: www.rowevetgroup.com

The Vale Veterinary Group

The Animal Hospital, Stinchcombe, Dursley. GL11 6AJ

Telephone: 01453 542092

Website: www.valevetsanimalhospital.co.uk

Twitter: @ValeVetsDursley

About Hearing Dogs for Deaf People

Hearing Dogs for Deaf People is a world leader in the training of hearing dogs, with each hearing dog helping to bring a visibility to their recipient's deafness thanks to the burgundy jackets they wear when out in public. For the past 30 years the charity has seen over 1,600 life-changing hearing dog partnerships created right across the UK.

Hearing dogs provide their recipients with independence, confidence and companionship by alerting them to important household sounds and danger signals such as the doorbell, telephone, cooker alarm, alarm clock and smoke alarm in the home, at work and in public buildings.

As well as alerting their deaf recipients to sounds, the burgundy jacket worn by hearing dogs when in public brings a visibility to deafness. Hearing dogs also help recipients overcome the isolation that deafness can bring.

Due to increased demand for hearing dogs from deaf people all over the UK, there is a continued need for funds to enable the Charity to increase the number of hearing dogs that can be trained each year.

Find out more on their website at: www.hearingdogs.org.uk or follow them on twitter at @hearingdogs.

...and a note from Rachael about what it's like to be deafened and NOT have a hearing dog.

The reason I'm so keen to support Hearing Dogs for Deaf People, is that one of the things that affected me probably more than anything was my loss of confidence, and with it a bit of my independence. Don't get me wrong - I'm very lucky - I'm not housebound, but since losing a large percentage of my hearing I've felt less happy about going out alone. I've been clipped by cars in car parks more times than I care to remember. I hate it when people drive up behind you and then sound their horn to make you move (often accompanied by angry faces, as they think I was doing it on purpose, or gales of laughter when they see me jump). I've developed a nervous 'tic' whilst crossing the road (you know how difficult it is to cross the road listening to an iPod) and I've had the horrible experience of people shouting at me for 'being ignorant' when I've failed to get out of their way.

It really does affect your confidence when you're out on your own and you can't hear traffic, or people coming up behind you, people on bikes etc. Only a few weeks ago Greg had to come and find me in a department store, as the fire alarm was going off and the tannoy was telling people to evacuate. I was oblivious and swooning over fabric. The alarm was so high pitched that I couldn't hear it, and the tannoy just sounded like static. Although you can make a joke of it, there's the very real 'what if it was a real fire, what if no-one had found me?'

My job means that I have to stay places overnight. I'll tell the people in reception that I'm hard of hearing and will need to be woken if the alarm goes off, then I tie myself up in knots wondering if they've any axe murderers masquerading as receptionists (I have a very vivid imagination). I often get the frights if I'm walking on my own. I've done one of the walks at Cirencester Water park in what is probably record time, because I realised I was a fair way from anywhere and couldn't see if there was anyone behind me, let alone hear. We practically sprinted it!

As well as the importance of alerting deaf people to danger signals, it's the visibility of hearing dogs that's also important. The Boy - many years ago - tore strips off a woman in a supermarket who had started shouting (at my back) about how ignorant I was, because I didn't stand aside so she could get past me with her trolley. Her reply to him was simple 'she doesn't look deaf - she should wear a badge or something'. If I'm going to have to start wearing a badge that says 'DEAF' then I've encountered a few people who are definitely going to need one that says 'STUPID'.

However, I understand the problem of not 'looking deaf' (I've had that said to me a time or two) so the maroon jacket worn by hearing dogs is a great way to alert others that we're not ignorant - we're just not very good at hearing. It's actually incredibly hurtful to be on the receiving end of someone showing off and loudly announcing to everyone else in the shop how rude you are. I'm not a shy retiring lass by any stretch of the imagination - yet I've fought back tears more than once when it's happened.

And the other side of the coin - whenever I've had to ask anyone for help, people are really kind, and go out of their way to look after you, either staying close and repeating announcements or checking you get on the right replacement train or bus. I've flown back to the UK on my own - it was scary - but if you do have hearing problems it's always worth letting the airline know as they will assign someone to look after you so you don't have to do the 'last one on board' walk of shame when you've missed the calls for your flight.

Anyway - before you all start feeling terribly sorry for me (there's really no need) - here's my favourite deaf story - it still makes me laugh. It's what happens when you ask a slightly tipsy person for help.

I was travelling back from London, and the train had been stopped for ages at Didcot. It was the last train so I was a bit nervous about missing my connection at Swindon. Across the aisle from me were a group of very smartly dressed business people. It looked like they were celebrating a good business win. The tannoy crackled into life with a muffled announcement, so I leant over and asked them what was being said, explaining that I couldn't hear very well.

The lady in the group told me that someone on the train had been taken ill and they were waiting for the paramedics to take them off the train.

The tannoy crackled again, and once again the lady looked over and explained that anyone travelling to Cheltenham need not worry as they were holding the train at Swindon. I thanked her and carried on reading my book and drinking my tea.

The tannoy crackled again. The lady leant over and said that the train manager was coming down the train and anyone who was travelling to Cheltenham should make themselves known to him. I thanked her again.

A few minutes later the train manager walked into our carriage, so I put up my hand and said

"I'm travelling to Cheltenham".

He looked down at his notepad, and before I could say another word, the lady pushed him out of the way, leant across the aisle to me and whilst miming someone writing, bellowed in a slow deliberate voice…

"HE'S WRITING IT DOWN"

Hot tea shot out of my nose.

FARMERS MARKETS

	THURSDAY	FRIDAY	SATURDAY	SUNDAY
WEEK 1	Mangotsfield Thornbury	Gloucester	Stroud	
WEEK 2	Stow-on-the-Wold Tewkesbury	Cheltenham Gloucester	Cirencester Dursley Stroud	
WEEK 3	Lechlade Thornbury	Gloucester	Berkeley Winchcombe Stroud	
WEEK 4		Cheltenham Gloucester	Cirencester Nailsworth Stroud	Bourton-on-the-Water

8126456R00100

Printed in Great Britain
by Amazon.co.uk, Ltd.,
Marston Gate.